WHY DIDN'T THEY TEACH ME THIS IN TEACHER'S COLLEGE

.... Or In Professional Development

R.S. Masterson

CONTENTS

Title Page
Introduction
Part 1: What is Learning?   1
Part 2: The Very Basics of Cognitive Science and Neuroscience (The Very Basics).   11
Part 3: Important Concepts For Learning   17
Part 4: Theory to practice   52
Part 5: Physical Classroom Environment - Catering to the 5 senses.   73
Part 6: A shared community   77
Part 7: Managing Behavior   83
Part 8: Homework   98
Part 9: Music and Learning   105
Continuing Education / Fact Checking   113
Free Resources Produced by Experts On the Current Body of the Science of Learning   115
Books   119
Courses   131
Teachers College Resources   135

INTRODUCTION

I want to start by clarifying that I am not a cognitive scientist or neuroscientist; I am a teacher and a practitioner in the field of teaching and learning. While my goal here is to communicate the science of learning and how it has positively impacted my teaching and learning, my primary focus has not always been that. My primary focus has always been on how the latest insights from experts in learning can inform my teaching and enhance my ability to positively impact my students. This is an ongoing process for me, and I will continue to push forward.

First and foremost, I'd like to address a common misconception among teachers, which is that many of these ideas that I'm discussing are theoretical and lack concrete proof. It's important to understand that just like gravity remains a "theory," these psychological and behavioral insights into learning are also considered "theories." The word theory doesn't mean there is no good evidence for something. These ideas, which I discuss in this book, have been rigorously tested and repeatedly validated across various scientific disciplines. They provide reliable frameworks for making predictions about learning outcomes with a high level of confidence. This is how all science operates, and the "theoretical" label should not deter us from utilizing these constructs to inform our practices.

I want to reiterate that most of the information I'm presenting here represents the current consensus of experts in the fields related to learning. As a non-expert, it's not my role to determine the accuracy of this information. My aim is to contextualize it in a way that is practical and beneficial for teaching. In fact, the most pressing need now is to bridge the gap between theory and practice, particularly by equipping teachers with these concepts and facilitating their implementation in everyday classrooms. This sharing of knowledge is precisely what I'm striving to achieve.

My primary audience for this book is teachers, but parents and students, or anyone looking to increase their knowledge about learning can benefit greatly as well. The concepts discussed in this book are derived from my personal research into effective teaching and my experiences in applying these concepts in my classroom. I chose the title of this book because it resonates with many individuals I've spoken to, including myself, who have wished that this type of knowledge had been part of their teacher training. The subtitle is a subtle critique of current teacher professional development, which, in my opinion, always falls short. The information I present in this book has had a monumental impact to my teaching and learning. My hope is that this book provides readers with a deeper understanding of how to become better teachers, improve their own learning, or support their children or students in their learning journeys.

PART 1: WHAT IS LEARNING?

This is a question that, in my experience, most teachers don't give a lot of thought to. If by chance it does come up, it is not given much thought or reflection, and it definitely is not an idea we use to change or modify what we do. In fact, I think it is just something that is taken for granted. We teach our standards or curriculum, and students learn.

The problem is that when you really try to think about what learning is and pull back the layers, you start to see that learning is not one thing or one simple process. Just by reflecting on it, it opens that can of worms that our education system is not prepared to address.

Let's start here by looking at some definitions of learning.

Merriam-Webster

1: the act or experience of one that learns.
2: knowledge or skill acquired by instruction or study.
3: modification of a behavioral tendency by experience (such as exposure to conditioning).

Make It Stick: The Science Of Successful Learning By Peter C. Brown, Henry L. Roediger Iii, Mark A. Mcdaniel

Acquiring knowledge and skills and <u>having them readily available from memory</u> so you can <u>make sense of future problems and opportunities.</u>

The Conditions Of Learning By Robert Gagne

"A change in human disposition or capability that <u>persists over a period of time</u> and is not simply ascribable to processes of growth."

Psychology Of Learning For Instruction By M. Driscoll

"We define learning as the transformative process of taking in information that—when <u>internalized and mixed with what we have experienced</u>—changes what we know and <u>builds on what we do</u>. It's based on <u>input, process, and reflection</u>. It is what changes us."

Connectivism: A Learning Theory For The Digital Age By George Siemens

"Learning is a process that occurs within nebulous environments of shifting core elements – <u>not entirely under the control of the individual.</u> Learning (defined as actionable knowledge) can reside outside of ourselves (within an organization or a database), is focused on connecting specialized information sets, and the connections that enable us to learn more are more important than our current state of knowing."

Richard E. Mayer From Learning In Encyclopaedia Of Educational Research.

"Learning is the <u>relatively permanent change in a person's knowledge</u> or behavior due to experience."

Ruth C. Clark & Richard E. Mayer. From Elearning And Science Of Instruction

"Learning involves <u>adding new information to your memory</u> and making sense of the presented materials by <u>attending to relevant information, mentally organizing it, and connecting it with what you already know.</u>"

Piaget's Constructionist Learning Theory

"Learning is defined as a process of <u>Individual construction of knowledge</u> 'from within' <u>through assimilation and accommodation of ideas.</u>"

As I have wrestled with this, I have come to the understanding that having a specific definition is not so important. What is important though is thinking about the important concepts that underlie these definitions. If you noticed, I underlined many ideas in the definitions that I think are important to expand on. Some of these may be familiar to you and some may not. I think they are all things that teachers should be familiar with, and use to help update their understanding of how they teach, what learning is, and how it happens.

Construction of knowledge

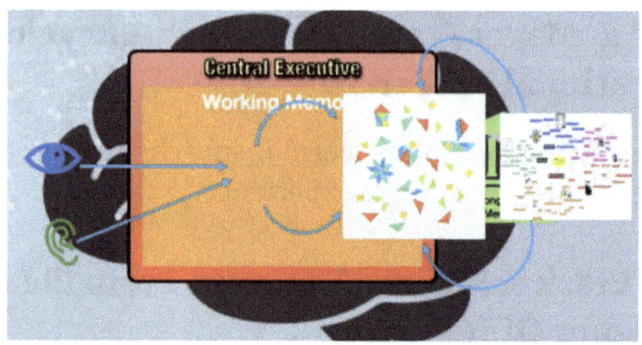

Knowledge is always being constructed. It means we build it up piece by piece with new learning being built on previous learning. This concept of constructing knowledge also has implications for how we remember things.

This blew me away the first time I learned this. Our knowledge is being reconstructed every time we remember it. It is not just being remembered like a static picture, but constantly reconstructed every time. Memories and knowledge are interconnected to other information in vast networks. These memories are different each time because it is literally "reconstructed" with whatever new information we have learned since the last time we recalled it. As you can see this can have some massive implications on how we think about our lessons, how we teach them, and how we try to connect students learning to other things they have learned. It also keeps me thinking about students background knowledge and experience and how important that is to what they are currently learning.

Assimilation and Accommodation

Put simply these are two pathways we have to classifying and organizing new knowledge.

Assimilation is the simple way and easy way. Students are taking new information and assimilating or classifying it according to their current schema that already exist. **Schema** are units of knowledge in the brain. They include the idea and many of the interconnected ideas related to it. I like to think about it like a web of interconnected information.

Let's think about how Assimilation might work. I want my students to learn about a new animal. Lets say they already know what a cat is.

Cat:
- 4 legs
- ears
- hair all over its body,
- it is a common pet.

Now I will introduce them to a new animal.

New Animal:
- 4 legs
- ears

- hair all over its body,
- it is a common pet.

The easy assimilation is that it is another cat. Now this may be true and is a good first step in thinking. But it is not always accurate.

Accommodation is the harder way of classifying and organizing knowledge. Accommodation is when you need to create a whole new category because the what you are learning doesn't quite fit with the current rules of your category. It is harder and takes more time and effort, but in the end is more accurate.

Cat:
- 4 legs
- ears
- hair all over its body,
- it is a common pet.
- **Meows**

New Animal:
- 4 legs
- ears
- hair all over its body,
- it is a common pet.
- **Barks**

This new animal doesn't quite generalize to a cat anymore. We will call this new animal a dog.

While my examples might be overly simplistic, it has helped me greatly think about and develop a more nuanced understanding of how students are learning and how easy it is for them to make inaccurate connections. Over time it can create some pretty significant misunderstandings. As a teacher it tells me that I need to push kids to take extra steps in their thinking. That is a natural for all of us to stop at assimilation. I have tested this many times over and over in my classroom and found it to be true on a daily basis. It helps me be more thoughtful, cautious, and diligent in my push to teach in more accurate and effective ways.

Internalizing Information

Learning is not just about remembering or retrieving information you learned. As I mentioned above, you don't just remember things you *reconstruct* it. Beyond retrieval you want to try to internalize knowledge by **reflecting** upon it and using it. This idea of reflecting is nebulous though and in my experience is rarely rarely specified just what actionable things students should be doing when they reflect beyond just thinking about it. A large part of reflecting should be doing something with the information. Some of these things might be:

- Organizing the information with other information.
- Assessing the information you have.
- Connecting the information to other information or

experiences.
- Asking questions like "why..? And how...?"
- Compare and contrast similarities and differences.
- Make connections to your own life.
- Breaking it down into smaller and smaller parts or steps.
- Try to think about goals or next steps based on the information.

Learning Happens Over Time

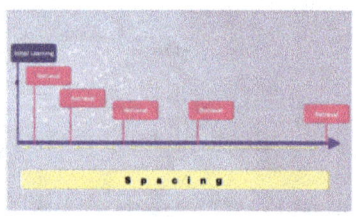 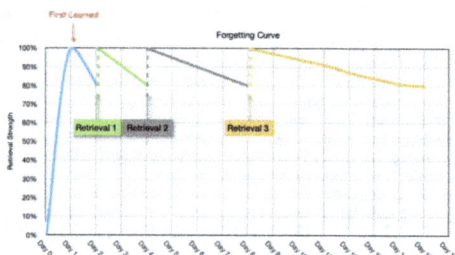

Learning is a gradual process that unfolds over time; it's not a one-time occurrence. During this process, information gradually becomes accessible from memory and endures over the long term. It's crucial to understand that this information isn't static; it is reconstructed. Another critical aspect is **forgetting**, which actually plays a vital role in learning.

Giving time for forgetting and employing spaced repetition is essential for effective learning. Spaced repetition, often referred to as "spiraling" in many curricula, is rarely discussed thoroughly in educational settings. Furthermore, from my experience, the way these curricula implement spiraling often requires significant teacher intervention to be effective.

Spacing helps because it allows for interference from related memories and reinforces connections when information is successfully recalled after intervals. The longer this successful recall occurs over spaced intervals, the stronger the memory becomes. This is especially important when considering that a part of learning involves applying information to solve future problems and seize opportunities in the real world, beyond the confines of a classroom.

Learning Is Not Entirely Under the Control of the Individual

In general, individuals are not particularly adept at learning. They often struggle to accurately assess their own knowledge , their **judgments of knowledge** are poor. They tend to overestimate what they know, they have an **illusion of knowledge**. As educators, we very often make the mistake of treating students as if they have already mastered a subject when, in reality, they are novices. It took me a while to grasp this concept, as it contradicted my initial beliefs about teaching when I was a younger teacher. However, especially with young students, they often lack the skills to guide their own learning effectively.

There's a common temptation to embrace approaches like "discovery learning" or "inquiry-based learning," which may seem appealing at first glance. However, when we delve deeper into the nature of learning, we discover that while independent learning can occur and can be powerful, it is often highly inefficient and can lead to significant misunderstandings. Moreover, these approaches tend to overlook one of humanity's greatest strengths: the ability to pass knowledge forward, allowing us to build upon previous knowledge. We don't need to reinvent the wheel every time we learn something new.

Another critical aspect of learning is testing. Unfortunately, testing has received a negative reputation due to its misuse. In reality, testing is one of the most valuable tools in our educational toolkit. However, many educators and education systems fail to use tests effectively, which means that students miss out on discovering the true power of tests as a learning tool. More on this later.

PART 2: THE VERY BASICS OF COGNITIVE SCIENCE AND NEUROSCIENCE (THE VERY BASICS).

I've often wondered why teacher training programs do not prioritize imparting a fundamental understanding of how the brain functions. Personally, I never received such training, and I've observed that many of my colleagues in the education field are in the same boat. Some argue that brain science is not essential for our role as educators, asserting that we are teachers, not neuroscientists. However, I strongly disagree with this perspective.

Education, much like many other fields, is not a singular, isolated domain. It requires drawing insights from various disciplines to support our work effectively. Among these relevant disciplines are neuroscience, psychology, behvaior science, and human and child development. While we don't need to become experts in all these fields, having a basic understanding of them is important as these are things teachers deal with on a day to day basis. The more knowledge we have of these areas only enhance our abilities as educators.

In this book, I want to establish the premise that having a basic understanding of how the brain works and how we think should be considered essential knowledge for teachers. My belief in this stems from my own experience: when I gained a rudimentary understanding of brain processes, it significantly improved my comprehension of various aspects of learning.

I want to clarify that I'm not claiming to be a neuroscientist or a cognitive psychologist. There's much more to memory and brain function than what I'll cover here. However, simply connecting the fundamental concepts of brain function to our teaching methods has had a profound impact on my effectiveness as a teacher. I believe it has the potential to make a substantial difference in the teaching practices of other educators as well.

Basics of Neuroscience

Neurons are the basic cells in the brain. They are made up of a cell body with a nucleus. There are dendrites which receive signals and there are axons that release or spread the signals to other cells. These neurons "fire" or send signals to other neurons.

Neurons will grow and search for connections to other neurons. More and more neurons connect together to form complex interconnected webs. These connections can be made stronger or weaker depending on when and how often they have been activated in the past. Active connections tend to get stronger, whereas those that aren't used get weaker and can eventually disappear entirely.

Essentially this is where memory begins, it is the reactivation of a specific group of neurons, formed from the strength of connections between neurons. Two things become important to me as a teacher when I think of this, the first is memory is based on the strength of the connection between "groups" or "networks" of neurons. "Use it or lose it" so to say. The second is that beyond just the strength, the pattern of how these groups of cells fire is important. Different combinations of firing can elicit different memories.

That is it for the neuroscience. There are more in depth understandings that could be helpful but honestly just that basic idea is enough to push us forward to the next level.

The Basics of Cognitive Science and Psychology

Our understanding of learning can be likened to a complex web of interconnected ideas. This perspective, drawn from neuroscience, helps us explore how our brains encode and utilize knowledge. When we think about something, it's not merely a singular concept but a node within a vast network of interconnected thoughts.

Take the word "house," for example. Each person's idea of a house is connected to a myriad of other related notions. You might be thinking of your own home, a picture of a house you've seen, or even a cartoon house. Even just thinking about your own house can have vastly different connections to it depending on what kind of house you have.

Within this web of associations lie details like color, windows, and the surroundings, sometimes vivid, sometimes on the periphery. Moreover, our thoughts don't stop at the initial concept; they flow down a particular path, leading us to consider other related ideas. These interconnected thoughts form what we call "schema."

Schema consists of interconnected ideas that relate to one another, creating webs of information that extend into other schema or networks of information. This concept is pivotal in understanding how we process and retrieve knowledge.

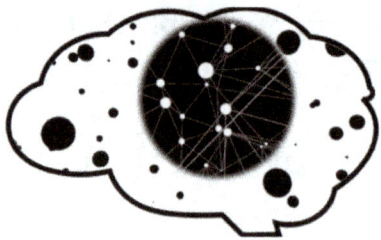

While schema is a concept that should be part of our daily conversations in education, it remains largely unknown among teachers and is seldom discussed. We touch upon it when discussing background knowledge and information connections, but we rarely delve into a practical understanding. This is why invoking "background knowledge" alone in educational discussions falls short, as we often neglect its profound connection to learning.

Perspective and situation play a crucial role in this concept and are essential elements in learning, yet they are often overlooked. Returning to the idea of schema, perspective and situation influence how information flows within these webs of interconnected ideas and the direction in which it moves to other schema.

As a teacher, recognizing that students encode and retrieve information through these interconnected webs has significantly influenced my daily teaching approach. Understanding that each student's situation and perspective are unique means they encode and access information differently, and it flows to various ideas differently. This awareness prompts me to be more considerate of the information I teach and how students' schema, their webs of interconnected ideas, may differ. It compels me to reflect on my own schema, addressing any gaps or assumptions that might not be evident to all students. It also emphasizes the importance of background knowledge and peripheral ideas that can be crucial for understanding new concepts.

Furthermore, it underscores the need to give students ample time to explain what they've learned, rather than assuming what they've grasped. Sometimes, students seem to grasp part of an idea, but further exploration reveals that their understanding has taken a different direction. In my view, this is akin to students stumbling upon related schema, but the flow of their thinking or the exact concept is not heading in the right direction. This could necessitate providing them with new information, introducing new schema or ideas, or altering the direction in which their thoughts flow between schema.

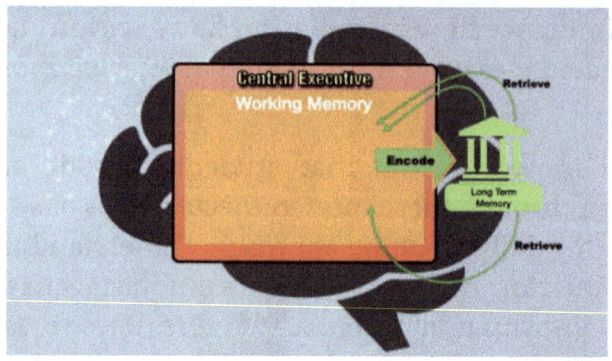

PART 3: IMPORTANT CONCEPTS FOR LEARNING

Rather than viewing memory as a static storage space for information, it's more beneficial to perceive it as a dynamic process involving the encoding and retrieval of information over time. While these are complex subjects, I'm providing a simplified overview that has greatly influenced my teaching, my students' learning, and my approach to education.

Specifically, I'm concentrating on two forms of memory: working memory and long-term memory. Understanding how these two types of memory interact can have a profound impact on both your teaching and your ability to learn effectively.

Long Term Memory

Long-term memory is precisely what it sounds like – it's the repository of information that has been effectively encoded into a schema, allowing us to retrieve it over an extended period. Essentially, it constitutes our background knowledge, a reservoir of what we've learned and remembered.

What's important to grasp is that long-term memories aren't static entities within the brain. When we recall something, we don't retrieve it exactly as we did before. Instead, each time we remember something, it undergoes a process of reconstruction. Every time we rebuild the memory, we are incorporating any new information that has been added or connected to it's schema since the last time you recalled it. This realization was quite mind-blowing for me and dramatically changed how I perceive the learning process.

Furthermore, it's crucial to understand that the reconstruction of each idea, memory, or concept can differ depending on the situation and context in which we're retrieving it. Imagine it as the flow from one schema to another, influenced by the specific context. This means that different situations can cause you to start from various entry points within your interconnected web of memories, leading to different emphases and paths of thought.

This newfound insight has prompted me to reevaluate my understanding of teaching. I now recognize that presenting information in a similar context and manner makes retrieval easier and strengthens recall. However, it's also important to acknowledge that not every learning situation can perfectly mimic what students have previously experienced. This can pose challenges, as students may think they're correct when their memory has been reconstructed inaccurately, incorporating new information that doesn't align with the old.

Moreover, it's essential to create diverse learning situations where students have to reconstruct information from different contexts. This process not only reinforces the retrieval process for that information but also strengthens the entire web of interconnected ideas, including surrounding schema. Ultimately, this facilitates more extensive knowledge transfer.

Teachers should also grasp the critical role that long-term memory (background knowledge) plays in helping us manage information within our working memory. Now, let's delve into working memory and why it's significant.

Working Memory

Working memory serves as the gateway for new information entering the brain, where it connects with existing knowledge stored in long-term memory. This information temporarily resides in working memory while you attempt to forge lasting connections and encode it more permanently in your memory. It's essential to avoid thinking of working memory as a static "storage" unit; instead, envision it as an active process. It functions by assimilating current environmental information and linking it to the pre-existing schema stored in long-term memory.

Sensory information from our various senses, such as sight, smell, touch, hearing, and taste, enters the brain. Before we consciously register it, this information undergoes subconscious filtering by what we call the Central Executive. This executive filter determines what information is relevant and what isn't, while also making subconscious connections with long-term memory. It predominantly filters out most incoming information and selects what's crucial for our focus. This process is why a student's background knowledge and experiences profoundly influence their attention and understanding of a lesson, often resulting in varying levels of comprehension among students in the same class.

It is critical to understand that working memory is extremely limited and varies from person to person. Generally, it can handle only a few "chunks" of information at a time, typically around 4 to 6 chunks. Defining a chunk precisely can vary from person to person, but for our purposes, consider it a small unit of information that working memory needs to process.

To illustrate this concept, consider numbers and letters as examples of chunks of information. If I give you a relatively short number, say 56437, you'll likely be able to recall it easily after a few seconds. If each number is a chunk, it is only five chunks. However, if I present you with a longer and more complex string, like 5903768yenjn, it becomes significantly harder to retain because your working memory can't hold such a large amount of information.

Crucially, both teachers and learners should understand that the process of focusing on new information doesn't occur in isolation; it happens while the real world continues around us. If our brain determines that something else is more important at the moment, such as needing to use the restroom, a noise in the hallway, or a friend's intriguing new pencil, it competes for space in our working memory. When this happens, you'll struggle to retain the information you're trying to learn. For teachers, this means that students won't successfully connect the new information to anything stored in long-term memory, hindering the learning process.

Cognitive Load and Overload

Cognitive Load refers to the amount of information that your working memory can effectively handle at a given moment. Keep in mind that this capacity is relatively small, generally accommodating around 4 to 6 chunks of information. Once you surpass this limit, you overload your cognitive capacity, leading to the loss of information. With this understanding, I've made a critical realization: students are constantly grappling with cognitive overload. This has been such an important realization can have a profound impact on teaching and learning. Several factors contribute to this:

- Limited Working Memory: Working memory is substantially more constrained than our curriculum and teaching often acknowledge.

- Inexperience with Learning: Younger students typically have less experience with learning, making it more challenging for them to manage cognitive load effectively.

- Lack of Background Knowledge: Students may lack the necessary background knowledge on specific subjects, adding to their cognitive load.

- Varied Working Memory Capacity: Working memory capacity varies among students; some have more limited capacity than others.

- Classroom Management: When a classroom is not managed well, it creates innumerable distractions. Creating a well-controlled classroom environment is paramount, particularly for younger students. A controlled environment minimizes distractions that could intrude on their working memory, allowing them to focus better.

- External Factors: Even with excellent classroom management, external factors like hunger, pain, strong emotions, or the need to use the restroom can influence working memory.

Working memory significantly impacts how students feel about learning, their classroom behavior, and their ability to absorb the material. This is especially pertinent for younger students who have less developed prefrontal cortexes – the part of the brain responsible for regulating thinking and emotions. Since the prefrontal cortex continues to develop until around age 25, younger students have even less control over their focus and attention, making the classroom environment pivotal to their learning.

Cognitive overload can lead to negative perceptions of learning in general or a specific topic. Students facing constant cognitive overload may become discouraged, act out, or develop a dislike for learning. Moreover, because they often don't understand why they're struggling, it can lead to negative self-perceptions, making them feel unintelligent or incapable compared to their peers.

Understanding cognitive load and its impact on working memory has enabled me to connect more deeply with my students. It's a constant consideration in my approach to their learning, from lesson planning to teaching itself. I continually adapt my methods to support my students and prevent cognitive overload, aiming to create a positive and successful learning environment year after year.

Chunking

Chunking is a crucial concept intertwined with our working memory and cognitive load. A chunk isn't a clearly defined thing; it varies based on the information and context. For new information, a chunk can be as small as a single number, letter, or symbol. If you've internalized information and formed numerous connections, a chunk might be more substantial, such as your friend's name, like "Chloe." Additionally, the context or your intended use of the information can influence what constitutes a chunk.

Organizing information into meaningful chunks has several advantages. It helps us make more connections, optimize space in our working memory, and provides greater opportunities for successful retrieval later on.

Let's revisit the example of numbers I provided earlier. "56437" was relatively easy to remember, and chunking wasn't necessary, although the brain may naturally break it into "564" and "37." Now, consider the more challenging string "5903768yenjn." Initially, it seems complex and devoid of meaning. However, when we reorganize it into chunks with more significance, such as "867-5309 Jenny," it becomes memorable, especially for those familiar with the famous song by Tommy Tutone. The first version would heavily burden working memory and require significant effort to learn, whereas the second version places minimal strain on working memory.

Let's explore one more pattern: "daecaibif." As one continuous string, it's challenging to remember. However, when we break it into more manageable chunks, like "dae cai bif," it becomes easier to recall. Now, consider viewing each chunk differently: "DEA CIA FBI." Suddenly, something seemingly meaningless gains profound significance, especially for those living in the US. Not only do each of these chunks acquire meaning, but their overall significance also becomes interconnected.

As a teacher, the deliberate organization of information into chunks has become a paramount consideration in my teaching methodology. Reflecting on how lessons are structured, how information can be chunked to span a unit, or how it can be laid out over years of learning has become a continuous source of opportunities for revision and improvement in my teaching approach.

Background Knowledge

Before I begin, I'd like to acknowledge that there are differences between "background knowledge" and "prior knowledge." However, for general educational purposes, I find that the distinction isn't particularly significant, so I often use the term "background knowledge" to encompass both concepts. I've found this broader interpretation to be enough, but I'm open to adopting more precise terminology in the future.

The concept of background knowledge has gained prominence, especially in the context of the Science of Reading, but its relevance extends far beyond reading. Let's break this down and explore why background knowledge is crucial for learning. I think of background knowledge as encompassing all the ideas and interconnected schemas that we can readily access. These pieces of information and processes have been encoded into our long-term memory and are retrievable. Importantly, they play a pivotal role in freeing up space within our working memory. Let's delve even deeper into this concept.

When information enters our working memory, our working memory draws upon our long-term memory, our background knowledge. Working memory strives to take this new information and connect it to our background knowledge, creating associations. This is an active process aimed at encoding the new information into an existing schema. You can visualize working memory being filled from both ends, and this is where background knowledge becomes essential. The more background knowledge you possess on a topic and the easier it is to access that knowledge, the less effort and space your working memory requires to process it. This, in turn, allows more cognitive resources and space in your working memory to be allocated to incoming new information.

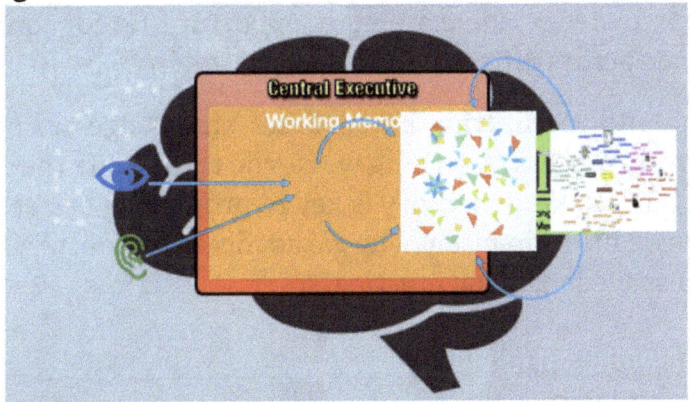

Consider the memorization of math facts as a prime example. When tackling math problems that involve multiple facts or require integration with other information, such as in word problems, if you don't have easy access to these math facts from long-term memory, your working memory will expend more effort and space to hold and process these facts. Consequently, other components of the problem may get displaced from working memory to make room for the math facts. This increases the stress, time, and effort required to solve the problem. Conversely, when these math facts are readily available and memorized, your working memory can concentrate on the other aspects of the problem.

Background knowledge also plays a critical role in knowledge **assimilation**. Without the appropriate background knowledge, dealing with new information becomes challenging because everything needs to be **accommodated**, meaning you must constantly create new categories or schemas for this information. This can easily lead to cognitive overload and result in the loss of the information you're attempting to learn. Essentially, it can feel like a backlog of information, and students may eventually give up out of frustration and exhaustion. Having a substantial background knowledge base also enhances a student's ability to transfer information to new areas. With more interconnected webs of knowledge, there are more opportunities for connections to be made across different knowledge domains.

Teaching and monitoring background knowledge are pivotal in the learning process. Anything we can do to alleviate the cognitive load on our working memory is key to promoting better learning outcomes. This is precisely why we advocate for mastery learning through spaced retrieval practice.

Memorization

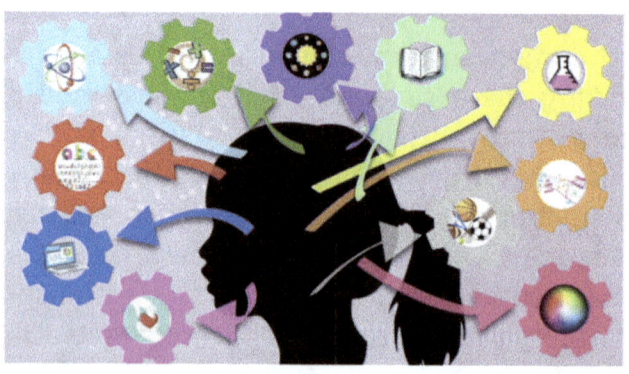

The topic of memorization has been a subject of ongoing debate in education, with arguments both in favor of and against its role in the learning process. At its essence, memorization involves the process of encoding facts and information into memory and subsequently retrieving them at a later time. This process shares commonalities with what is known as retrieval practice, as it requires individuals to actively extract information from memory, contributing to the learning process.

Learning occurs through the act of retrieving information and making sense of it. Initially, the recalled information may seem rigid, like disparate puzzle pieces coming together to form a complete picture. However, with continued retrieval practice, the memorized content becomes more adaptable, enabling its application to novel situations and problem-solving scenarios.

It's important to note that while memorization of information is not the ultimate objective of education, it holds significance in many educational contexts. Researchers who specialize in the study of learning processes have discovered that a deeper reservoir of factual knowledge enhances one's capacity to engage in critical and analytical thinking. In essence, memorizing facts lays the groundwork for higher-order thinking and effective problem-solving skills. Consequently, memorization contributes to the development of a more efficient memory system, transcending the limitations of memory capacity and duration.

What distinguishes memorization from true learning is the presence of meaning. When you memorize a fact, it often appears arbitrary and interchangeable; whether it's the capital of a state or a simple multiplication like 2 x 10, it may seem to hold little significance on its own. However, it's essential to remember that memorization is retrieval and retrieval isn't something that happens in isolation. Instead, it involves the active engagement of your cognitive faculties. When you memorize (encode and retrieve) a fact, you are, in fact, learning it, and it becomes intricately connected to other pieces of information within your mental framework.

To illustrate this concept, let's consider a specific example: the process of memorizing basic math facts. This process goes beyond mere rote learning, as it serves a more profound purpose. For instance, when you commit to memory that 2 x 10 equals 20, it forms a vital component within a larger cognitive schema in your brain. This fact becomes integrated with other thoughts and ideas, creating a foundational connecting point for comprehending related concepts. As you progress through your educational journey, you will encounter various instances where the number 20 reappears, such as when you learn that 4 x 5 also equals 20. These interconnected webs of information form a robust foundation for understanding and building upon your knowledge as you continue to learn and experience more complex mathematical concepts and beyond.

10 + 10 | 25 - 5 | 30 - 10 | 20 x 1 | 22 - 2 | 18 + 2 | 40 / 2 | 24 - 4 | 19 + 1 | 17 + 3 | 20 + 0 | 16 + 4 | 11 + 14 - 5 | 14 + 6 | 23 - 3 | 13 + 7 | 21 - 1 | 27 - 10 + 3 | 28 - 8 | 26 - 6 | 29 - 9 | 2 x 2 x 5 | 8 + 12 | 9 + 11 | 6 + 14

All of these expressions result in the sum of 20. It's important to recognize that each of these mathematical operations isn't just an isolated piece of information; rather, they contribute to the development of our numerical understanding. As we engage with these mathematical concepts, we gradually construct connections that expand our overall knowledge of numbers.

This is where the concept of balance becomes crucial. Memorization serves as an initial step in building these fundamental connections, allowing us to encode and retrieve information effectively. Subsequently, the process of learning, which involves making connections, reflection, and practice, further enhances our ability to link these points together and foster the growth of our knowledge.

The key takeaway here is that without this foundational information, the deeper understanding of mathematical concepts becomes challenging to achieve. Contrary to the notion that memorization hinders critical and analytical thinking, it actually forms the bedrock upon which these advanced cognitive skills are built. Moreover, the process of memorization need not be dull or monotonous; it can be engaging and intellectually stimulating.

As we'll delve into later, removing stress and high stakes from practicing math facts can actually transform it into an enjoyable activity. We'll explore this idea in more detail shortly, but in essence, it taps into the same pathways in our brains associated with the pleasure of playing video games. Math facts, at their core, present straightforward problems, but when you increase their quantity and introduce a time constraint, they become a challenge. Completing each problem triggers a release of chemicals in the brain, leading to a sense of reward and satisfaction. This sense of achievement accumulates with each successfully completed problem.

Where we often stumble in education, in contrast to the success of video games, is in maintaining a delicate balance of struggle. Student need the right amount of success and failure. Students need to constantly feel they are on the cusp of success, just a bit more practice or a few more rounds away from reaching their goals. This is where the concept of "desirable difficulties" or "zones of difficulty," often referred to as "zones of proximal development," becomes significant. It involves ensuring that students are challenged and experience some degree of struggle, but not to the extent that they become discouraged or give up.

It's important to clarify that the disagreement regarding memorization is not rooted in a disbelief in the importance or necessity of memory. Instead, it revolves around the idea that understanding alone can naturally lead to the formation of memories without a deliberate effort to commit information to memory and practice retrieving it. Additionally, there's a misconception that memorization is antagonistic to creativity and innovation.

Unfortunately, many teachers hold a mistaken belief that encouraging students to remember information is unnecessary in today's digital age. They often say things like, "Why bother remembering it when they can simply Google it?" These educators have been trained to prioritize what are perceived as "higher-order skills," such as critical analysis and synthesis, while dismissing what they consider "lower-order" skills like memorization and comprehension of factual information.

This perspective has given rise to significant challenges in the field of education, as evidenced by the ongoing reading reform movement. For an extended period, the prevailing approach emphasized instruction in reading comprehension "skills," including activities like "making inferences," often sidelining the acquisition of foundational information. It has become increasingly clear that this approach was flawed. Nowadays, there is a growing realization that students must learn and memorize phonics patterns to develop strong reading skills. Additionally, building a foundation of "background knowledge" around various subjects is essential for students to grasp them at a deeper level.

It is crucial to emphasize that memorization does not hinder creativity or innovation; rather, it serves as the bedrock of these processes. Creativity and innovation require a base of information to build upon. In elementary education, this dynamic is readily observable. In a common classroom activity that demands higher-order thinking skills, success often hinges on whether students possess prior knowledge. Those who already have the necessary background knowledge tend to excel, while those without struggle and often gain little from the task.

This situation is disheartening for two reasons. Firstly, students who struggle may receive praise for their effort or creativity during the task, which may create a false sense of achievement. However, this facade is shattered when they are confronted with the need to continually acquire more knowledge on top of the basic skills they lack. In essence, this approach compounds challenges for these students in the long run, impeding their overall educational progress.

There are two additional arguments I'd like to address briefly. The first argument often asserts that we can rely on Google for information in today's digital age, which is indeed a powerful resource. However, this argument becomes less convincing when we consider the vast amount of essential knowledge that cannot be simply Googled. If we were to depend entirely on Google for everything, it would consume an impractical amount of time, leaving little room for other tasks and endeavors. The reality is that we all utilize Google to some extent, regardless of our existing knowledge. Rather than seeing Google as a replacement for learning, we should view it as a tool to enhance our understanding and tackle more complex challenges. The more information we know the more we can use it to push our understandings to newer and higher levels. Thus, the argument for Google should ultimately serve as an argument for acquiring more knowledge independently and using Google to extend our capabilities.

The second argument I'd like to address is the notion that goes something like, "I never learned my math facts, and I turned out just fine." While it's true that you may have turned out fine, this argument overlooks the counterfactual scenario. Yes, you are doing well, but what if you had learned your math facts? Would you have received a better education, pursued more opportunities, or achieved even greater success? The absence of an experience or skill doesn't necessarily imply that you wouldn't have benefited from it. It's crucial to encourage self-reflection, both for ourselves and our students, and recognize that different choices could have led to different outcomes in our lives. This kind of introspection can guide us toward making informed decisions for the future.

The core issue, and perhaps what led us to this point, is the recognition that learning extends beyond mere memorization. While memorization serves as a foundational step, true learning involves taking that acquired knowledge and applying higher-order thinking skills to engage with it. This entails breaking down information, making connections, and conducting analysis and synthesis.

The complexity of learning emerges when you take information you've memorized or retrieved from memory and then engage in a process of analysis and synthesis. Notably, many time the "other information" with which you connect to must also be something you have already have in your memory. Other times might involve integrating new information to old information, the key lies in your ability to link this fresh knowledge to previously acquired information through something like analysis and synthesis. This interplay between existing and new information enhances the depth of learning, promoting a richer understanding of the subject matter.

Mastery vs. Non-Mastery

To effectively address the crucial issue of background knowledge, we need to delve into the concept of Mastery Learning versus Non-Mastery Learning. There seems to be some confusion around this topic, often related to a misunderstanding of the concept of "spiraling" in curriculum planning. Some educators believe that merely introducing information over time through spiraling will eventually lead to comprehension. While this approach may work in some cases, the key missing piece is that students must establish initial connections before spiraling becomes effective. They need to demonstrate that they have encoded and can retrieve the information, as well as made meaningful connections before we transition to spiraling. I'll elaborate on this when discussing **spacing** and **retrieval practice.**

As I've refined my understanding of how learning occurs, it has become evident that we should adopt a mastery-focused approach to student learning. However, it's essential to recognize that achieving mastery requires more time and effort. We should revisit the fundamental concepts discussed earlier: that learning is an incremental process and that we don't have complete control over it. Merely encoding information into long-term memory doesn't mark the end of our teaching journey. Information is woven into complex webs of knowledge, and the strength of these connections can diminish over time, impeding recall. Additionally, it's crucial to ensure that the information we teach is initially encoded effectively.

Here's how I approach this:

Anticipate Background Knowledge Needs: Before starting a new school year, a unit, or a lesson, it's essential to consider what background knowledge students will require. This planning phase is critical for ensuring that students can build upon their existing knowledge as the year progresses.

Connect New Material to Background Knowledge: When introducing a new topic, I strive to connect it to relevant background knowledge. However, this can be challenging as students often have varying levels of prior knowledge. Identifying which students need more support in acquiring this background knowledge is crucial. Knowing this in advance helps me incorporate appropriate background knowledge throughout the year.

Immediate Assessment: Right after teaching, it's essential to assess all students to determine who successfully encoded the information and who didn't. This step is crucial because even with careful teaching, not all students will grasp the material initially.

Gradual Release: I employ a gradual release approach, moving students toward independence at their own pace. Those who understand the material proceed to more scaffolded or worked examples, while those who require additional support receive immediate reteaching. Various teaching methods, such as worksheets, centers, group work, or pairs, can facilitate this gradual release process.

Spacing and Retrieval Practice: Learning isn't instantaneous, and students don't have complete control over their learning. Even if students initially grasp a concept, it doesn't guarantee long-term retention. Therefore, it's crucial to strengthen these connections over time. This involves consistent reteaching as a natural part of the teaching and learning cycle. Additionally, revisiting previously taught concepts over time and gradually increasing the intervals between recalls is essential. This may involve integrating practice problems into subsequent lessons, assigning homework, creating quizzes, conducting cumulative reviews, and administering tests throughout the unit and year.

It's worth noting that many students may lack essential background knowledge altogether, which is a systemic issue in our education system. In response, I have found success in taking my time to build this background knowledge by selectively choosing what to teach, even if it means skipping certain topics. By prioritizing the teaching of critical concepts and ensuring student success in these areas, we not only help students learn important material but also boost their confidence and enthusiasm for learning.

Novice vs. Expert Thinking:

To understand the concept more clearly, we should recognize that our level of expertise in a particular subject significantly impacts how much working memory we require. Experts in a field need less working memory to process and connect information, allowing them to allocate more cognitive resources elsewhere. Conversely, novices use most, if not all, of their working memory to absorb new information and make connections with it. When we consider students as learners, they are inherently novices in the subject matter they are studying. This applies regardless of their age or the context of their learning.

To illustrate this point, let's use the example of trying to learn a new language. Even if you possess well-developed study habits and learning techniques, you can't think like an expert in that language because you lack the experience and background knowledge necessary to do so.

Therefore, it's crucial for teachers to understand how easy it is for a student's working memory, particularly that of a novice thinker, to become overwhelmed.

In a school setting, especially at the younger grade levels, students are not experts in any subject. They are novices both in terms of learning in general and the specific topic being introduced. Treating them as experts can lead to adverse consequences. Let's delve deeper into this distinction between expert and novice thinking:

Teachers are experts in what they teach, especially from the perspective of their students. This expertise is due to the accumulation of knowledge and experiences over time. By the time someone becomes an adult, they have gained an extensive understanding of most subjects taught at elementary and middle school levels. Additionally, adults possess a wide range of life experiences that contribute to their comprehensive understanding, including self-control, understanding consequences, and the purpose of learning. These experiences form an intricate web of knowledge, allowing for a more complex comprehension of what is being taught.

On the other hand, students, as novices, lack the mental resources and schema that teachers have. They may struggle to comprehend complex concepts and patterns that experts take for granted. They can easily make inaccurate assumptions and come to the wrong conclusions. Novices require explicit, step-by-step instructions to make sense of new information. They need guidance to build on their prior knowledge and connect the dots in a subject.

Take, for instance, the elementary math problem 15 + 27. Novice thinking involves counting on fingers or using basic counting methods, such as counting by ones or tens. This approach takes more time and places a heavy load on working memory, increasing the likelihood of errors. Novices often lack solid foundational skills, such as number sense and basic addition facts, and may miss out on fundamental concepts like place value.

Novice Solution: (Counting by ones) 15, 16, 17, ..., 40, 41, 42.

Moreover, constant cognitive overload can be stressful and demotivating for novices, especially if they make mistakes despite putting in considerable effort.

Expert thinkers, in contrast, have a deep understanding of addition, have memorized basic addition facts, and employ efficient strategies based on place value and base 10 operations. They can quickly arrive at the correct answer, with less cognitive strain and lower chances of error.

The distinction between novice and expert learning is important, but it can be further complicated by teaching methods like discovery learning, inquiry-based learning, and project-based learning. While these approaches offer valuable learning experiences, they can be inefficient when specific content needs to be taught. Novice learners often lack the skills to guide themselves effectively and may struggle to identify their mistakes. Additionally, the notion of "reinventing the wheel" suggests that we don't need every student to rediscover existing knowledge independently. Instead, we can share our accumulated wisdom to help them build upon it.

This is not to say that discovery learning and similar approaches lack value; they have their merits when used appropriately and for specific purposes. However, it's essential to consider the pros and cons of each approach and use them thoughtfully.

Forgetting

To truly grasp the intricacies of memory and cognition, we must address a fundamental yet often unknown aspect: **forgetting**. While it might seem counterintuitive in the context of learning, forgetting plays a pivotal role in effective cognitive processing and learning. This often-neglected topic holds immense significance for how we approach education, teaching methods, and curriculum design.

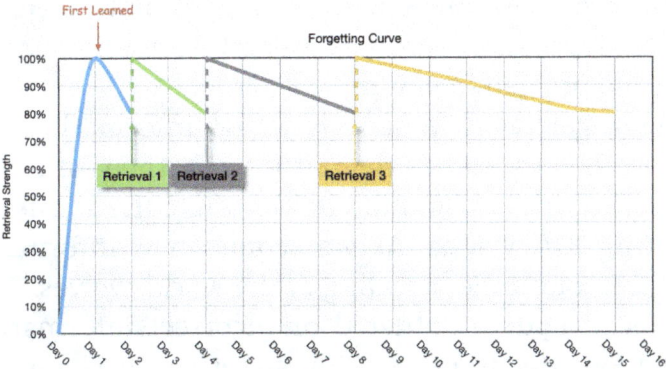

Consider the process of learning once more: our working memory attempts to process an array of external information simultaneously. However, working memory has severe limitations and cannot handle this information overload. Consequently, it must be selective in the data it chooses to focus on. Once information is prioritized in working memory, it undergoes either assimilation into existing mental frameworks (a relatively straightforward process) or accommodation into entirely new mental categories (a more challenging endeavor).

However, encoding information into memory doesn't guarantee its long-term retention. We've all experienced instances where we knew something at one point, only to forget it later—akin to the "use it or lose it" adage. Additionally, we encounter those frustrating "tip of the tongue" moments where we sense we possess knowledge but can't quite retrieve it. Forgetting is an inherent and natural aspect of the learning process, concealing deeper implications than meet the eye.

Before delving into the reasons why forgetting holds such importance in learning, let's briefly outline some key factors. Then, we'll explore the why behind its significance:

- **Selective Memory**: Not all information we encounter is equally valuable or relevant at all times. Forgetting helps our brains prioritize important information by discarding less important or outdated details. This selective memory process ensures that we retain the most relevant and useful information for decision-making and problem-solving.
- **Efficient Retrieval**: When we forget information and later relearn it, the process of relearning strengthens and reinforces that fact that this information is relevant to use at this time.
- **Updating Knowledge**: As we acquire new information and experiences, our understanding of the world evolves. Forgetting allows us to update outdated or incorrect information. This updating process is crucial for adapting to changes in our environment and keeping our understanding of the world current.
- **Avoiding Interference**: Forgetting helps prevent interference between similar pieces of information. If we retained every detail we ever encountered, our memories would become cluttered and intertwined. Forgetting minimizes the risk of such interference and allows us to better differentiate between

similar concepts.
- **Adaptive Memory**: Forgetting promotes adaptability. Our memory system is optimized for retaining information that's most relevant to our current circumstances. What's important today might not be as relevant in the future, so forgetting ensures that our memory storage remains flexible and adaptable to changing needs.
- **Encouraging Active Processing**: The act of forgetting and subsequently relearning stimulates active processing of information. When we encounter information for the second time, our brain engages in deeper processing, which enhances comprehension and retention. This deeper processing often involves connecting new information to existing knowledge, leading to a richer and more interconnected memory network.
- **Overcoming Cognitive Load**: Constantly retaining all information can lead to cognitive overload, making it difficult to focus and think clearly. Forgetting helps manage this cognitive load by allowing us to prioritize and concentrate on the most relevant information at any given moment.

Forgetting constitutes an integral facet of the learning process, serving several vital functions. It allows our brains to function efficiently by filtering out less pertinent information, enhancing memory through the process of relearning, facilitating knowledge updates, averting interference, adapting to novel situations, fostering active mental processing, and managing cognitive load. Acknowledging forgetting as an inherent element of learning can lead to more proficient and streamlined cognitive functioning.

Retrieval Strength and Storage Strength:

There are two key components involved in memory: **retrieval strength and storage strength**. These concepts help us understand both how memories are initially stored and how they can be later accessed.

Retrieval strength pertains to how easily and readily a memory can be recalled from long-term memory, especially in specific contexts like during a test. Memories with higher retrieval strength are more likely to be remembered under specific circumstances. Factors influencing retrieval strength include recent exposure to the information, contextual cues, and the number of associations or connections the memory has with other related information. You can think of retrieval strength as how readily accessible a piece of information is to you.

On the other hand, **storage strength** refers to how deeply a memory is encoded, determining the likelihood of being able to recall it over time. Memories with higher storage strength are better retained in the long term. Factors contributing to storage strength include the depth of processing during encoding, the emotional significance of the memory, and the amount of rehearsal or repetition involved.

Here is a common and easily digestible example you can find when you are looking for examples of retrieval and storage strength:

		Retrieval Strength	
		Low	High
Storage Strength	High	Childhood phone number.	Current Phone Number
	Low	Hotel room number from last year	Current hotel room number.

Here I have put it in a classroom context:

		Retrieval Strength	
		Low	High
Storage Strength	High	Yesterday I memorized my math multiplication facts for 6's. The next day I am struggling to complete a timed test. I remember them but I am slow to recall them or need a hint/cue. I know what vowels are consonants are but when I try to use them in phonics or recognize them, I get confused and need time to think.	I learned my math facts last year and I am continuing to use them everyday in math to solve harder problems more efficiently. I learned about vowel teams earlier in the year and I am able to recognize and read words fluently with various vowel teams in them.
	Low	My teacher just taught a lesson on the multiplication of 6's but I was focused on time. I was hungry and can't wait for lunch. Now I can't remember what he said. I am trying to learn learn about multi-syllable words, but I am still struggling with basic alphabetic principle. I can't seem to remember anything.	Studied my math facts right before a test. My teacher just taught a lesson on what a vowel team is and immediately after the lesson I need answer some questions where I pick out vowel teams within words.

Several variables come into play when considering storage and retrieval strength. Factors such as time, practice (repeated repetitions), context, emotional impact, and more can influence these strengths.

It's possible to learn something once and have both high retrieval and high storage, meaning you can easily remember and retain the information. Conversely, attempting to learn something repeatedly over an extended period may result in continued difficulty in recalling and retaining it.

Understanding these concepts becomes particularly crucial for teachers when they're considering prior knowledge, planning lessons, and fostering the development of knowledge in their students.

Transfer of Knowledge

The recurring theme of knowledge transfer is pervasive in pedagogical discourse, where the acquisition of knowledge in one situation prompts its application in another. Though the notion appears conceptually simple, its practical manifestation proves considerably more complex. To really understand this, we need to delve into some of the intricacies of the cognitive processes behind transferring information.

We start with information entering into the working memory. Subsequent encoding and consolidation processes strengthen and reinforce the neural connections pertaining to this information, affording it greater retrieval and storage strength. This process allows for establish contextual links within cognitive schemas, forming the foundation for knowledge transfer. From here a critical aspect of knowledge transfer resides in fostering inter-schema connections. This highlights the necessity of deliberate retrieval practices across diverse environments and in conjunction with varying other schema. Moreover, it also requires us to build up our background knowledge in other areas so that we are able to make those connections.

We generally talk about transferring knowledge in two ways:

1. Near Transfer: This refers to applying information in similar contexts, which is generally considered easier.

2. Far Transfer: This involves using information in novel or different contexts, which is typically more challenging.

However it is important to acknowledge thinking about knowledge transfer as near and far, is inaccurate and problematic. It is really a continuum, where each individual's continuum is unique, predicated on the distinct background knowledge and experience they bring to the table. Ultimately, for every bit of information, each person will fall on different parts of the transfer continuum differently based on their background knowledge and experiences.

This really starts to highlight why students from different backgrounds or who have different amounts of experience in life don't always fare as well in academic situations. This should emphasis the importance for building common background knowledge in school before we teach.

Next I'd like to point out that the intricacies of transferring knowledge can be deceivingly complex, especially for someone who has expert knowledge of a topic.

To illustrate this, let's consider two contrasting elementary scenarios: one involving near transfer and the other, far transfer.

Near:

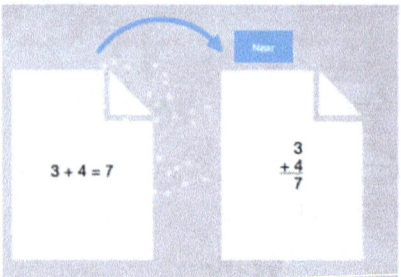

In the "near" example, we categorize it as near transfer because almost everything remains identical between the two situations: the paper, the numbers, and the equation. The knowledge required in the first scenario is essentially the same as that needed in the second, with one key difference. In the latter, the student simply needs to recognize that the direction of the equation has changed. At these very basic levels, something as seemingly minor as this can be enough to confuse novice students. To an expert, it is hard to even conceive of this being a problem.

Far:

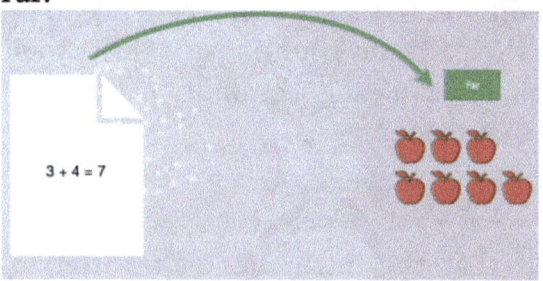

In the second "far" example, we label it as far transfer due to the numerous dissimilarities between the two situations. The first example involves numeric values within an equation, while the latter presents physical objects (apples) with no numerical representation. In this case, the students must transfer their understanding of the number 3, representing three objects (the apples), and the number 4 representing four apples. The addition symbol signifies the combination of all the apples, and the equals sign represents the resulting count of 7 apples.

It's important to note that the information required to comprehend the near situation differs significantly from that needed in the far. While these distinctions may appear minor to adults, experts, they can pose significant challenges for children, novices, in the learning process. Additionally, what qualifies as near or far transfer varies among individuals, and the degree of proximity or remoteness in the transfer also varies.

A series of very small steps.

A series of very gradual steps form the foundation of my teaching approach. In particular, the initial steps hold significant insight.

Step 1: Encoding and Independent Replication: In this initial phase, the objective is to impart a concept to students and subsequently gauge their individual comprehension. It's crucial to recognize that since knowledge transfer varies among individuals, every student must independently demonstrate their understanding. Relying on one student's response as proof of collective comprehension is not best practice. To achieve this, I may employ methods such as having students repeat the concept or solve a problem either on a whiteboard or in a notebook. This process essentially serves as a replication of the same task, confirming that knowledge has effectively transferred. For example, if my goal is to teach sentence writing with a capital letter at the beginning, I would initially present a sentence like "The dog is happy," erase it, and then request that the students reproduce the exact sentence to confirm their understanding. When some students fail to capitalize the first letter, it becomes evident that knowledge transfer has not occurred, prompting the necessity for reteaching. It's worth noting that this replication, though sometimes perceived as mere copying, represents the initial phase of learning—a pivotal step before delving into further contextualization. This principle also applies to mathematics. If I solve a problem in a specific manner, I would ask the students to solve the exact same problem.

This aspect is generally overlooked by educators who assume that doing the same problem doesn't equate to comprehension. However, it's important to recognize that many students may still lack understanding. By having them tackle the same problem, it reveals specific areas where their comprehension falls short, enabling immediate re-teaching to bridge the gaps before progressing to the next phase of knowledge transfer.

Replication is the first step of learning. Do what I do before we put it in a different context.

Step 2: Independent Replication in a New Setting: During this phase, students are assigned the task of reproducing a similar or even the same problem. However, what makes this phase noteworthy is that they do so after a brief pause or spacing event, or they work in a different physical location. This shift, be it from the carpet to their desks or from their notebook to a worksheet, introduces a spacing event that necessitates the transfer of knowledge from one context to another. It's at this point that students often encounter difficulties in recalling the information recently taught. This transition holds educational significance primarily due to two factors: retrieval and spacing. It represents a challenging facet of teaching and learning, particularly considering the novice status of the learners. As experts, it can be challenging for us to appreciate how these minor alterations can impact novices, but they unquestionably do. To underscore this, consider the analogy of language learning. Even seasoned educators, when learning something entirely new like a foreign language, may experience a similar phenomenon. They might initially comprehend a concept when taught, only to later sit down to write a sentence in their notebook and find that the knowledge has seemingly vanished from their memory.

Step 3: Similar But Different, and Repeat: This phase represents our true endeavor to facilitate knowledge transfer as commonly understood in educational contexts. Students need to repeat similar problems that have minor alterations. The Repetition of these minority different problems plays a pivotal role here, as each iteration enhances retrieval and storage strength. Additionally, the repetition of these "slightly different problems" gradually incorporates new schemas into the retrieval process, broadening the students' conceptual understanding and allowing for further transfer.

Step 4: Spacing, Interleaving, and Retrieval: This is where the strengthening and broadening of connections intensify. Considerable time is allocated, potentially in varying environments, to reinforce learning. Waiting a day or introducing interleaved practice are strategies that can further enhance knowledge retention. Moreover, assigning homework proves valuable when executed thoughtfully. It introduces both spacing and a new environment for retrieval, challenging students to recall information without the familiar cues of the classroom. This process also exposes students to diverse schemas, fostering the development of expansive neural networks that facilitate broader knowledge transfer.

Subsequently, educators should continue to space out the information through out the year and over multiple years while introducing new contexts for retrieval. This ongoing approach paves the way for successful knowledge transfer.

Multitasking

At this point I'd like to quickly highlight an important truth: multitasking is not a reality. Our working memory is severely limited, and it simply cannot handle focusing on more than one task simultaneously. Even if we possess a substantial amount of background knowledge that may free up some working memory, our attention remains directed at a single task. What we're actually capable of is task switching.

The ease with which we can switch between tasks depends on various factors, including the number of connections we've made to the information, its storage strength, and retrieval strength. If you find this idea challenging to accept, I encourage you to take a few minutes to research it. The existing studies are quite interesting and conclusive.

The key takeaway here is that we shouldn't encourage the idea of multitasking in classrooms. Educational environments, especially, require students to concentrate on their learning. Promoting multitasking can only hinder their progress, potentially leading to a situation where students overload their working memories.

Engaging Students Does Not Equal Learning

It's crucial to understand that mere engagement doesn't guarantee learning. The fact that a student appears engaged doesn't always indicate that they are absorbing and comprehending the material. This misunderstanding can be a persistent source of frustration. While it's true that engagement is a component of the learning process, and I concur that increased engagement often correlates with improved learning outcomes, we tend to overly prioritize the creation of "engaging activities."

Let's examine a few examples that illustrate how the appearance of engagement can be deceptive.

Example 1: You give a quiz in Social Studies about the 50 states with a class. The students are having a great time competing with each other and are very engaged.

The purpose of this activity is to help them practice naming each of the 50 states based on the shape of the state. Zoe is loving this activity and competing with her friends. In her mind, she if focused on beating her other friend Ahmed.

Each time her focus switches to her friend Ahmed to see if she beat him or not, but is not focused on if her answers are right or wrong.

Her focus is not on retrieving and making connections to the information, but on the competition. So she is engaged but focused on the wrong thing.

Example 2: You are doing a lesson on subtraction and you are

subtracting apples. You bring in apples for the students to manipulate and eat afterward. One of your students didn't have breakfast. He is very engaged on the apples but his focus is on his hunger and not on the subtraction. He may be engaged but might night retain the information because he is focused on his hunger and not the subtraction.

Example 3: A teacher puts a lot of funny gifs in their presentation on geometry because they know the kids love them and it keeps them engaged. But the gifs don't really connect to geometry.

Each time she comes to one of the gifs, the kids are so engaged. They laugh and talk about it. But when the presentation is finished, they only remember the gifs and not the information. Their working memory was so focused on the fun but unrelated stuff, that it didn't take in the knowledge the teacher wanted them to. They were engaged on the wrong information.

These are what are called "**seductive details**." These are intriguing pieces of information that, although interesting, aren't relevant to achieving the instructional objective. We sometimes include them because they're exciting, and we want our content to appear more engaging. However, what often occurs is that students become "engaged" with these details, but they divert their attention away from the actual learning target. In other words, seductive details end up distracting students from the core learning objectives.

In fact many times learning doesn't need to be exciting. A student may not be fully engaged or find a lesson particularly entertaining, but they can still grasp the intended knowledge or skills. They were disengaged in terms of enjoyment but managed to learn.

While creating engaging educational materials is important, it should come secondary to a specific process:

1. First, concentrate on determining what needs to be learned and how you will assess whether learning has occurred or not, which involves defining your assessment criteria.

2. Once you've established how to assess learning effectively, you can then design engaging and enjoyable ways to involve students in the learning process.

PART 4: THEORY TO PRACTICE

First, let's clarify our goals for our students. What we ultimately want is for them to learn. To understand this better, let's revisit some of those fundamental concepts related to learning we talked about earlier:

Learning involves:

- Having readily accessible information in memory to make sense of future challenges and opportunities.
- Persisting over a period of time, meaning it stays in our brain.
- Internalizing and blending with our experiences.
- Building upon what we already know.
- Involving input, processing, and reflection.
- Not being entirely under the individual's control.
- Resulting in a relatively permanent change in a person's

knowledge.
- Adding new information to memory.
- Paying attention to relevant information, mentally organizing it, and connecting it with existing knowledge.
- Individually constructing knowledge through assimilation and accommodation of ideas.

If our aim is for a student to master addition, for example, we want them to possess enduring, readily accessible knowledge. This implies the need to develop both storage and retrieval strengths. We want them to store the information securely and have the ability to retrieve it effortlessly when needed, allowing them to build upon this knowledge and adapt it to new situations.

When considering the practical application of these concepts in teaching and learning, it often feels like the key to effective education lies in understanding and applying three crucial concepts: retrieval practice, spacing, and interleaving. While each of these concepts is intriguing on its own, it's the synergy between them that holds the utmost significance.

Retrieval Practice

Retrieval practice involves actively recalling information from memory, a concept closely tied to the idea of desirable difficulties coined by Elizabeth and Robert Bjork. It's not merely reviewing; it's an active process of trying to remember.

Effective retrieval practices include:

Summarization: Restate the main ideas of a lesson or retell the key parts of a story.

- Brain Dump: Set a timer, jot down all you know about a topic on paper or a whiteboard.
- Mapping: Create a mind map connecting related phrases or ideas.

- Drawing: Illustrate the concepts you're learning.
- Frequent Low-Stakes Tests: Administer regular, low-pressure tests on the subject.
- Test Creation: Develop a test based on your knowledge.
- Elaboration: Explain things to yourself, asking questions like "why" and "how."
- Teaching: Share what you've learned with someone else.
- Enacting: Act out the information you've acquired.

Just to be clear retrieval practice is not things like:
- Highlighting
- Rereading

Why is retrieval practice so important?

The ultimate goal of learning is to allow us to access and apply information as needed. To achieve this, we rely on two essential factors: strong retrieval strength and strong storage strength. To understand how our brain handles new information, let's break it down. Initially, our working memory encodes this information and establishes connections with our existing knowledge, but these initial connections typically have limited retrieval and storage strength.

To bolster this pathway, we must actively encourage our brain to reinforce it. Additionally, we should fortify the surrounding connections to ensure that multiple pathways for retrieval are strong and abundant. This is where retrieval practice comes into play.

Without retrieval practice, the learning process becomes considerably more challenging. If we merely study or learn something once, our retrieval and storage strength remain weak. We fail to signal to our brain that this information is vital to retain, diverting its efforts towards strengthening other connections. Eventually we forget to the point that retrieval is not possible. If we resort to mere rereading or highlighting, we miss the opportunity to engage in the active recall of specific information. This lack of effortful recall diminishes the strength of the connection, as our brain is being given the information again, it is not being asked to retrieve the information.

A common modern-day illustration is our reliance on phones for storing phone numbers and directions. In the pre-smartphone era, we memorized numerous phone numbers and could navigate without relying on maps. We had to actively recall and use this information from memory.

However, with the advent of smartphones, these tasks have become automated. We're either provided with the information or it's done for us, leading to a decrease in both retrieval strength (our ability to recall) and storage strength (our ability to retain) for these details.

Spacing

This concept is straightforward: it involves spacing out the intervals between recall events. Ideally, you should gradually extend the time between each retrieval event while also varying the conditions and environments in which you retrieve the information.

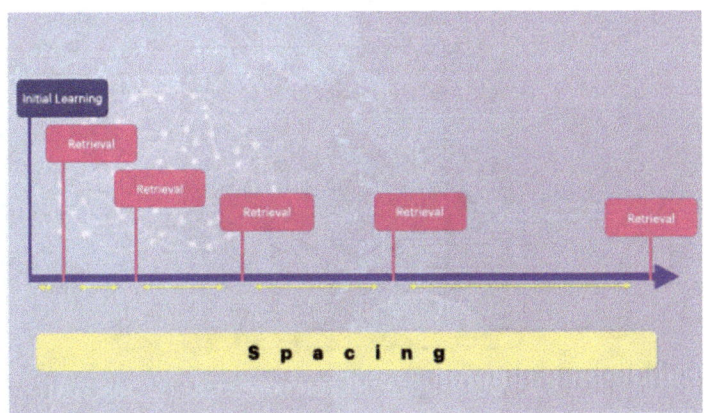

Why is spacing so important?

Retrieving something once signifies a momentary high retrieval strength, which is typically what we think of in a classroom setting. It's like saying, "I've taught you this concept, now demonstrate that you understood what I taught." However, this initial retrieval strength does not last. If you don't use it you lose it. Our goal isn't for students to grasp something just temporarily; we want them to retain it for future use, achieving both high retrieval and high storage strength. This is where both retrieval and spacing come in.

To understand this better, it's essential to distinguish between encoding and consolidation.

Memory encoding is the initial formation of a node and connections within a schema.

Memory consolidation is the process of strengthening and broadening these connections, making future retrieval easier. Another way to think about it is consolidation is the brains way of maximizing storage space. Things that are not used are diminished in importance. Things that are used are given priority.

In education, we often place a strong emphasis on the initial process of encoding while inadvertently neglecting the crucial step of consolidation. This tendency arises because we typically follow a pattern of teaching a concept and then moving on to the next one. I understand that this is generally more a result of a curriculum that is out of our control, but it further emphasizes why teachers need more of a say in what we teach. The concept of spacing further highlights the need for us, as educators, to have more control and actively integrate and plan spaced events in our teaching practices.

Spacing involves deliberately allowing some degree of forgetting to take place and then revisiting the information after a period. This deliberate act sends a signal to our brain, essentially saying, "This information is essential; remember it." Furthermore, spacing allows us to reconstruct this knowledge in various contexts and situations, activating new connections each time we retrieve it. This increased connectivity enhances our ability to link it with additional information and apply it in diverse scenarios.

Repeated retrieval practice plays a pivotal role in strengthening recall over time. The more you engage in retrieving content, the better you'll remember, comprehend, and apply it.

Another critical aspect of retrieval and spacing that pertains us as educators is creating "successful" recall events. We must strive to create "successful" recall events while providing critical feedback. There are several compelling reasons for this. Firstly, successful recall reinforces the signal to that specific information, strengthening the associated pathways. The combination of successful retrieval and positive feedback not only enhances these pathways but also triggers a release of chemicals in the brain associated with happiness, fostering a positive learning experience associated with this information.

Conversely, if students recall information incorrectly and we fail to correct them, they may inadvertently strengthen pathways related to incorrect information. Once encoded, this can make it more challenging in the long run to relearn the correct version. Finally, a lack of opportunities for successful retrieval can lead to a loss of motivation and confidence among students. This, in turn, can create negative emotions related to learning and the subject matter. This is where scaffolding and cueing becomes invaluable. Ultimately, the goal is for students to perform without assistance, but scaffolding and cueing initially provide the support needed for successful retrieval, maintaining confidence and motivation.

It is important to note that sleep plays a crucial role in memory consolidation. During certain stages of sleep, the brain appears to be highly active in consolidating memories. It is during these periods that memories are integrated and organized, which can enhance their retention. For example, if you learn something new during the day, your brain may work on consolidating and strengthening that memory while you sleep. This is another important reason why schools and teachers need to learning about, emphasize, and inform students and families about good sleep habits.

Interleaving
Interleaving is the mixing of different topics or types of problems within a single study session. Instead of focusing on one topic or problem type at a time, which is known as "blocked" practice,

interleaving requires you to switch between different topics or problem types during your learning session.

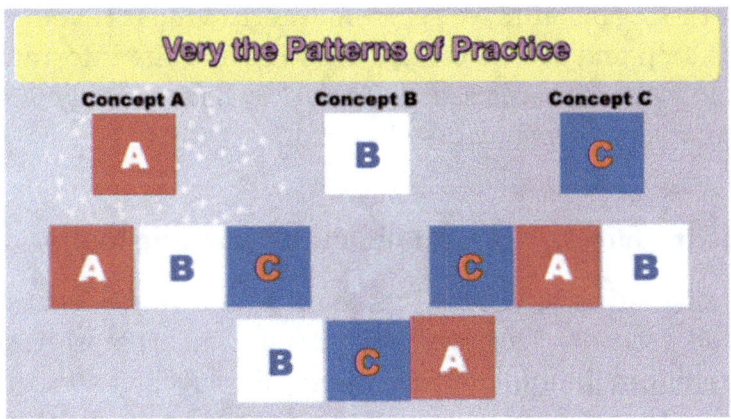

Why is interleaving so important?

Interleaving is essentially the practice of combining spaced repetition with repeated retrieval exercises of different topics at once time. It involves consistently challenging yourself to recall information in a mixed fashion, interspersed with various background knowledge, thus activating different schema. The dynamic interplay between these interleaved concepts serves to solidify new information while fostering broader connections.

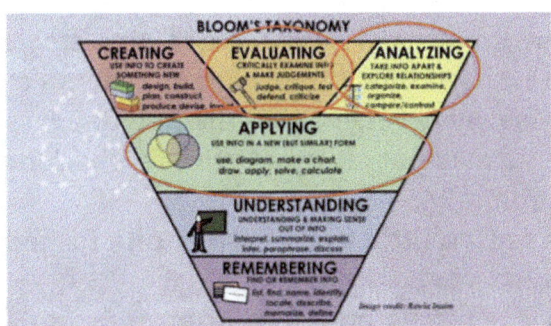

As time progresses, this approach yields several benefits,

including enhanced comprehension, improved pattern recognition, and a more profound understanding of the fundamental principles that link seemingly unrelated concepts.

One of the big benefits we get from Interleaving is that our brains have to stop and evaluate their thinking and the information by analyzing what is being asked. Then they have to apply what they know to make a decision on what to do.

The testing effect: The most important learning tool we neglect.

Tests and testing have often received criticism in education, and for valid reasons. The way we typically incorporate tests into education can be quite problematic. However, it's essential to recognize that testing is potentially one of the most potent tools in our teaching toolkit. Let's delve into this by defining what a test is.

A test is essentially a scenario where you're tasked with recalling knowledge or executing a task based on what you've learned previously. This assessment evaluates your competence, skills, knowledge, or other relevant attributes within a particular context or situation.

Now, let's break down the problems with the way we do testing in education:

1. Tests are typically administered in high-stakes situations.
2. Every test has a direct impact on a student's overall grade.
3. Students may never even see their grade.
4. Students may not always receive feedback or see their test scores promptly.
5. There's often little to no opportunity for reflection on the test results.
6. Once a test is done, we often move forward without revisiting the content, giving students only a single chance to demonstrate their understanding.

This approach to testing has given rise to a culture marked by confusion, wasted time, and subpar teaching:

1. Tests are commonly perceived negatively by both students and educators.
2. Test-taking becomes a source of excessive stress for students.
3. The primary focus tends to be on the superficial grade received, such as pass/fail or letter grades like A, B, C, D...., or percentages like 100%, 75%, 50%.....
4. Test quality may be lacking, with assessments failing to accurately measure what was taught.
5. Testing is often rushed and confined to the testing event itself, leaving no room for post-assessment assessment, reflection, reteaching, or retesting.

The problem lies in our how we implement tests and how we use tests in education. It is easy to see why it has garnered such a negative reputation in education.

Let's look closer into how we can harness the Testing Effect in education to improve our teaching and students learning.

The Testing Effect

The testing effect, also known as test-enhanced learning, refers to the improved long-term retention of information that occurs when learners **actively recall** or retrieve information from memory during the learning process. Does this sound familiar? The "effect' from the testing effect as retrieval practices, because a test is very useful form of retrieval practice.

However, when we typically engage in testing in educational settings, we often employ it at a basic level, as a one-time retrieval event. The true potential of "the testing effect", which is at it's core retrieval practices, is fully realized when it is combined with spaced and interleaved repetition. This approach helps us overcome the inherent imperfections in how our brains encode, consolidate, and retrieve information.

Regrettably, the most valuable aspects of the testing effect tend to be overlooked in traditional educational practices. In essence, we are underutilizing our most potent tool for learning.

The most effective way to take advantage of the "testing effect" involves repeated, low-stakes retrieval practices that are integrated into the learning process. These practices not only benefit students but also provide valuable feedback to teachers, guiding them on what steps to take next in the teaching process.

Why is the "testing" better than other retrieval practices?

I don't believe testing is universally superior in every educational scenario, but I do consider it the most vital and effective tool in our teaching toolkit for the majority of situations. There are several compelling reasons for this viewpoint.

Firstly, testing serves as a roadmap for our teaching. When starting on a new unit or lesson, it's crucial to begin with a clear end goal in mind, a clear purpose. We need to envision what success looks like and identify the essential steps students must take to reach that goal. Clarity and attainability are paramount. Unfortunately, some tests seem designed to "trick" students with questions that deviate from what they've learned. Such tests are unhelpful to everyone involved. My personal experience in graduate school taught me the frustration of receiving vague guidance without examples. It made me realize that, as a teacher, I want my students to have clear objectives and a well-defined path to achieve them. As a teacher, I also want to gauge whether what I've taught is actually being learned. From a student's perspective, knowing precisely what's expected of me allows me to direct my efforts toward productive learning.

Secondly, tests, when properly crafted, serve as targeted retrieval practice. Different types of tests align with distinct learning goals. An end-unit test assesses what was covered in that unit, while an exit ticket informs me if the day's lesson objectives were met. Review tests help gauge how well students retain previously learned material and whether I need to revisit specific topics.

Thirdly, tests offer opportunities for assessment and reflection. They generate clear and specific data that can swiftly guide both teachers and students toward their next steps. This assessment process helps dispel the "Illusion of knowledge" that some students may hold, and the subsequent reflection allows for another chance to think about the information and for students to internalize the information and make meaningful connections.

Finally, tests can take various forms to scaffold information effectively. At the outset, I may choose to employ formats such as True/False tests, scaffolded fill-in-the-blank tests, or multiple-choice tests to provide students with support as they grasp new concepts. As students become more proficient, I can challenge them with harder formats like short answer or long-form answer tests.

Testing and it's "testing effect" undeniably plays a crucial role in the teaching and learning process due to its ability to provide clarity, targeted practice, assessment, reflection, and adaptable scaffolding.

How should we implement "tests" in a classroom:

Let's begin by addressing an essential point: tests, quizzes, exit tickets, and similar terms all essentially revolve around the same core idea—they are all forms of retrieval practice. Although retrieval practice can encompass more than just these specific activities, it's crucial to recognize that these terms essentially describe the same fundamental concept.

This clarification holds significant importance for a couple of reasons. Firstly, it benefits teachers. Often, educators can become caught up in terminology like "formative assessment," "summative assessment," "exit ticket," or "quiz," which can unnecessarily complicate an already muddy educational experience. The truth is, they all provide the same powerful "testing effect" when executed correctly. While some tests may be lower stakes and some higher stakes, in terms of grades, they should all be approached the same way. No test is an "end". Test should act as roadmaps for teachers, offering focused retrieval practice that can be critically evaluated, providing specific data to guide both teachers and students in assessing the effectiveness of teaching and learning and determining the next steps, even if it is the end of a unit.

Secondly, this clarification serves the interests of students. As students progress in their learning journey, they will encounter these various terms, and it's crucial to prevent any potential confusion. What I want them to understand is that, regardless of the label, each of these activities represents a valuable learning opportunity. Students should be equipped to approach these situations effectively, comprehend what they can gain from them, and navigate their learning journey accordingly based on their experiences.

Going forward, whether I use the terms "test," "retrieval practice," "quiz," or any other equivalent term, I'm essentially referring to the same fundamental concept.

The Teaching and Learning Cycle: Teaching, Testing, Assessment, Feedback, Reflection, Meta-Cognition, Repeated Testing.

Let's delve into what is often referred to as "The Teaching and Learning Cycle," a concept many of you may already be familiar with. An important point to stress is that the initial encounter with a test should not be a high-stakes summative assessment, and the first mention of a test shouldn't automatically imply a high-pressure situation.

Regardless of the type of test involved, there are several universal aspects to this process that hold significance. Every test should include an assessment and reflection with the addition of feedback, empowering students to contemplate the results and make informed decisions about their next steps.

At first glance, this may seem like a complex and time-consuming process, but it doesn't have to be. In fact, **it often shouldn't be**. While we should allocate time for it more frequently, the actual time required should be minimal, with substantial benefits.

However, one crucial prerequisite is that students must be explicitly instructed in this process. They need to learn how to effectively manage and utilize it independently.

Let's break this down the teaching and learning cycle into parts:

Teaching: We should be beginning with the assessments in mind. Backwards designing our teaching to meet the specific goal we set. Set up important pretests, exit tickets, retrieval practices, that help to build up to the final test for the unit or lesson. Students should be made aware that this is the process we are taking so there is clarity from the start.

Testing: This is the testing part we have discussed. We give a test both as a a retrieval practice and as a way to determine how students are doing with the information.

Assessment: When referring to assessment here, I'm talking about marking answers as right or wrong on a test. Students should know how they performed for several reasons. Retrieval practice loses much of its value, if not all, without some form of assessment. The assessment of the activity informs students about what they understand and where they need improvement.

It allows them to correct mistakes, reflect on their strengths and weaknesses, and decide where they require further practice. Assessment, in itself, constitutes a type of feedback and naturally leads to meta-cognition.

The real challenge lies in the way we've structured the testing culture in education. Often, we restrict students' ability to engage in this natural process. This is where concepts like "Growth Mindset" become relevant. While "Growth Mindset" may carry some negative connotations, it can be effectively employed in learning contexts. Explicitly explaining to students that testing is a process and they are in one phase of it is crucial. We should convey that test results do not define them as good or bad students but simply provide insight into what they know and what they need more practice with. By encouraging students to examine which questions they answered correctly or incorrectly and prompting them to ponder "What does this mean?" and "What should I do next?" we foster a growth mindset. This process also encompasses meta-cognition and reflection steps.

Another essential aspect of assessment is its role in dispelling the **"illusion of knowledge"** and improving students' "judgments of knowledge."

- **Illusion of knowledge:** This term refers to a cognitive bias where students believe they possess a deeper or more accurate understanding of a topic than they actually do. This is a common occurrence in education. Recognizing this phenomenon can help address situations such as:

Overconfidence: Students may exhibit excessive confidence in their ability to explain or apply a concept, even when their understanding is superficial or incomplete

Resistance to Correction: When presented with new information or corrections, students may resist or become defensive because they believe they already possess accurate knowledge.

- **Judgments of Learning (JOL's):** These are meta-cognitive assessments individuals make about their own learning or memory processes. We continually make JOLs in learning environments. The issue is that JOLs are influenced by an individual's perception of their memory and learning abilities. As mentioned earlier, students, especially younger ones, are "novices" in terms of learning, with limited life and background knowledge to draw upon. Furthermore, all students are "novices" in the subject matter they are attempting to learn. This means they are often not good at accurately "judging" their own learning. However, this skill can improve with practice.

To reiterate, ensuring that assessment (marking answers as right or wrong) is viewed as a process in learning is crucial for effective learning. Assessment also serves to counter the "illusion of knowledge" and enhance students' "judgments of knowledge."

Feedback: The primary point to emphasize here is that feedback can be concise and swift. Once students have been guided to think about the what the assessment tells them, the assessment itself serves as feedback in most cases. This is often sufficient. Of course, in certain situations, more detailed feedback is appropriate. Feedback can be either immediate or delayed, with both approaches having their merits for different reasons.

Immediate feedback: This type of feedback enables you to promptly address the illusion of knowledge and correct inaccurate judgments of learning. It can lead to "Ah-ha" moments, immediately rectify misunderstandings, boost a student's confidence, or prevent negative thoughts if their performance was subpar, thus reinforcing a growth mindset.

Delayed feedback: This type of feedback offers a natural spacing effect and an additional retrieval practice session when it is provided. It can also deliver many of the same benefits as immediate feedback, but if there's been a significant gap between the test and the feedback, there might be a disconnect with the information.

Reflection: Similar to feedback, reflection can be straightforward and quick in most cases. Once students have been guided to think about what the assessment means and what it tells you, this act of thinking itself constitutes "reflection" and usually occurs automatically or with minimal prompting. However, there are instances, much like feedback, where more extended and involved reflection is valuable. The key takeaway is that reflection doesn't have to be complex or time-consuming.

Meta-cognition: In essence, explicitly teaching and encouraging students to navigate the teaching and learning cycle is a way of imparting meta-cognition skills.

Let's take a closer look at various types of tests and how they can be used effectively in the teaching and learning process.

Pretests: To be honest, I don't typically gather a lot of valuable information from pretests. Usually, pretests serve more as a tool for the students themselves. The purpose of this kind of test should serve two main objectives:

First, it introduces students to what they are expected to learn and provides them with a clear picture of the learning goals and outcomes.

Second, it establishes a starting point for students. At the end of the learning experience, they can compare their performance on the "post-test" to the results of the pretest and see how much progress they've made. This is especially valuable for students who may have faced challenges during the lesson. Even if their performance on the post-test isn't stellar, you can still encourage them by pointing out areas of improvement. Simultaneously, you can identify aspects they can continue working on. Essentially, it becomes a reflective learning event.

Frequent Low-Stakes Tests: Again it doesn't matter what you class these tests, "formative assessments, exit tickets, quizzes". What's crucial here is that they are administered frequently, have low stakes (or minimal impact on grades), and include a feedback and reflection component.

Varying the format of these assessments creates different contexts and environments for each retrieval practice session. You can also create a spectrum, starting with easier retrieval formats like "true/false," "multiple-choice," and "scaffolded formats" at the beginning and gradually moving toward more challenging formats such as short answer and non-scaffolded formats. Other formats, like "brain dumps" where students write down everything they know about a topic, and "summary points" where they jot down important lesson takeaways, can also be valuable. However, keep in mind that these activities can be time-consuming and still require some form of assessment, feedback, and reflection to be truly effective. Misinformation or misunderstandings can easily creep in without proper oversight.

Varying the stakes is equally important. While most retrieval practices should be low-stakes / no-stakes, no all should carry the same weight. Some should be medium stakes and a very few should be high-stakes. Having a mix that spans the range between low and high stakes can help students adapt their behaviors and approaches to different situations. It can also support students who struggle with test anxiety. Eliminating high-stakes tests entirely isn't advisable, as life will always present high-stakes situations where students need experience. Providing these experiences in a safe and structured educational environment is crucial for their normal learning and development.

Post-Tests: Post-tests hold significance for me because they provide a roadmap for where I want students to be and what I should be teaching toward. In fact, post-tests should serve as a starting point and guide for my teaching plan throughout a unit.

Ideally, a post-test should offer insights into the specific learning objectives and teaching points for the unit. Unfortunately, I often find that teaching points within units can be too vague, inconsistent, and open to interpretation, making it difficult to accurately assess learning outcomes in the end. A post-test should inform me of what needs to be taught and how to teach it effectively. If I cannot accurately assess what has been learned, then the entire educational process becomes less effective.

Ultimately, my primary goal, and I hope this holds true for every teacher, is to see my students perform well, or to the best of their abilities, on the test. The test serves as a reflection not only of the students' learning but also of my teaching effectiveness. While a post-test typically carries higher stakes and contributes to their grades, both students and teachers should understand that it is not, or at least should not be, the endpoint of our educational journey. Instead, we should view it as a tool for reflecting on our progress and contemplating our future learning paths.

Let's be perfectly clear: testing is essentially a form of retrieval practice. While some people may wisely attempt to distinguish between the two terms, there's a fundamental similarity between them. In reality, the distinction lies in how we conduct testing, which can significantly impact the learning process. I believe that by attempting to separate these terms, we may inadvertently create more confusion and obscure the critical details. Personally, my aim is to reshape my students' perception of testing. I want them to perceive testing as a valuable learning strategy and gain a better understanding of its role in the educational context.

How I try to set up a positive environment for retrieval practice in my classroom.

My approach to tests at the beginning of the year typically goes something like this:

"In this class, we'll be regularly taking tests—every day, in fact. These tests will vary in size, with some being small, others medium-sized, and occasionally, we'll have bigger ones. Let's delve into what a test actually is. A test is a form of retrieval practice, and I'll take some time to explain this concept, which we'll be using throughout the year. Essentially, it's a tool we use to gauge what we know. After taking a test, we can assess whether we knew the material or not. This process is important and incredible for several reasons:

- The most exciting aspect is that just taking the test itself helps us learn. It's a form of retrieval practice, so whether we already knew the information or not, it remains a valuable learning activity.
- Tests help clarify misunderstandings. For instance, they might reveal, 'Oh, I thought it was this, but now I see it's actually that.'
- They provide guidance on what to do next:
    - Retry if needed.
    - Practice more if required.
    - Move on to more challenging topics when ready.
- Tests shatter our illusion of knowledge (a term I'll explain and use throughout the year), making us recognize our limitations.
- They prompt us to re-examine and adjust our judgments of

knowledge (another term I'll delve into and utilize throughout the year).

The first several days and weeks I will review specifically the teaching and learning cycle. I will be very explicit on working through each part of the teaching and learning cycle and what students should do. It's important to give lots of opportunities for successful assessments, while at the same time walking through what happens when you are unsuccessful. This is setting up the "growth mindset" that we need students to have. As the year progresses, I make sure to continually review these steps, providing reminders and highlighting successful events at each step.

PART 5: PHYSICAL CLASSROOM ENVIRONMENT - CATERING TO THE 5 SENSES.

Considering the classroom environment is crucial but often overlooked. This applies to all age groups, not just younger students. The more inviting a classroom is, the more conducive it becomes for learning. This concept addresses fundamental human needs such as safety, consistency, a sense of belonging, and comfort. To meet these needs, I've adopted a strategy that focuses on engaging all five senses.

Sight: It's important for the classroom to have an appealing visual aspect. While everyone has their own style preferences, there are some general principles to consider.

1. Clean and organized setup: A well-organized classroom is welcoming and provides a sense of consistency and stability, which may be lacking in some students' home environments.

2. Appropriate lighting: Lighting plays a crucial role, with natural lighting being ideal. However, it's important to accommodate varying preferences. Some students prefer brighter lighting, while others prefer dimmer settings. A good compromise is to start with slightly dimmed lighting at the beginning of class and gradually brighten it as the work begins. Lighting also influences the classroom's mood; dimmer lighting often creates a calmer atmosphere. Depending on your situation, you can consider bringing in adjustable lamps to cater to individual preferences.

3. Colors and decorations: Here, personal preference comes into play, and it's possible to overdo it. However, adding some color, patterns, and tasteful decorations can enhance the classroom's inviting and enjoyable atmosphere. Incorporating pictures or posters that contribute to a welcoming environment can be beneficial. While "academic posters" may not always be effective, their usefulness depends on how they are utilized. Personally, I prefer decorating my room with themes like the solar system and nature scenes.

Sound: This aspect holds significant importance in creating the right classroom atmosphere. While I will go a little deeper on music later, I'll provide a brief overview here.

1. Music and Relaxing Sounds: Music or soothing sounds such as waves, water, or wind can greatly contribute

to a welcoming, relaxing, and comfortable environment. Different types of music or sounds can be employed to set various moods for different purposes. For instance, upbeat music can infuse excitement, but it should be used judiciously to avoid overwhelming the environment.

2. Background Music as White Noise: Using music as a form of "white noise" to mask other sounds is worth considering. In particularly noisy school or environmental settings, employing music or background sounds to drown out distractions can be highly effective. Using a consistent, familiar sound that students become accustomed to can be particularly helpful in some cases. When faced with the choice between chaotic, unpredictable external noise and controlled background noise that aids in blocking out disturbances, opting for the latter is often the better option.

Temperature: This is often beyond our control, but I address it by having an open discussion with students and encouraging them to wear comfortable clothing. Research has shed light on what constitutes a comfortable environment, although it was conducted with adults in an office setting, the findings are insightful. The studies indicated that women tend to be most comfortable and productive at around 75 degrees, while men perform best and are most comfortable at 70 degrees. I think we can even move beyond gender and safely say, different individuals have varying temperature preferences for optimal productivity. As a teacher, this motivates me to advise students to be prepared, whether it's by wearing layers of clothing they can adjust or bring to class because temperature can impact their learning.

Dealing with a cold room is relatively straightforward; I encourage and allow students to bring long sleeves, sweaters, or sweatshirts. In some cases, I suggest students bring warm water or tea (depending on their preferences).

However, managing a hot or humid room is more challenging. I've taken measures such as bringing in electric fans to help regulate the temperature, especially during the summer. Additionally, I encourage students to wear appropriate, cool attire and ensure they have access to cold water. As an elementary school teacher I have the luxury to prohibit drinks like soda and juice.

Smell: A pleasant aroma in the room contributes significantly to its welcoming atmosphere. Every year, I receive compliments from both students and parents about how delightful the room smells. It's a simple aspect that can be easily adjusted if it has a negative effect on students.

To achieve this, I use various methods:

1. Plugins: I prefer automatic spray air fresheners that can be set on a timer. While they are the pricier option, I find them to be the most effective.

2. Aerosols: I typically keep a can or two in my room and give a light spray every morning to maintain a consistent and pleasant environment as students arrive.

3. Gel-based air fresheners: These are the most budget-friendly and convenient option, and they are my go-to choice. They can usually be found for about a dollar each or even less. I place two or three in the room at a time, and they typically last for about 2-3 weeks.

Taste: Taste and smell are closely connected, but when it comes to taste, I have one key piece of advice. Keep some delicious treats on hand to distribute as you see fit. Personally, I'm not against it, and I've never encountered a student who objected to a tasty reward.

PART 6: A SHARED COMMUNITY

In contemporary teaching, a significant focus revolves around creating inclusive classrooms and showing respect for every student. This is a vast and complex topic that I won't delve deeply into here. Instead, I'd like to discuss two approaches I've found particularly effective in fostering a sense of community among students.

Classroom Jobs:

I firmly believe in assigning responsibilities to each student in the class. While this strategy is most suitable for elementary and some middle school settings, I believe there are innovative methods to adapt it for middle and high school classrooms too. The central idea here is to emphasize that every student has a role within the classroom community, and everyone's participation is essential and valued.

One common challenge I've noticed is that many teachers find it difficult to establish a cohesive classroom community when implementing this approach. Allow me to clarify that what I'm suggesting is not a straightforward endeavor. Beyond simply defining the roles, the real challenge lies in effectively managing students while they carry out these responsibilities. Some teachers opt for assigning roles like "teacher's helper," "whiteboard cleaner," or "paper passer-outer" to the most responsible students, which can indeed lighten the teacher's workload but often falls short of fostering a strong sense of community within the classroom.

Furthermore, some educators may hesitate to entrust responsibilities to challenging or disorganized students due to trust issues and the necessity for constant supervision. It's undeniably a demanding task, but I cannot stress enough how frequently delegating such responsibilities to such students has resulted in improved behavior over the long term.

Here are some valuable insights I've accumulated over the years concerning the assignment of classroom responsibilities:

1. Provide tasks that are manageable and take time to coach and help students to accomplish those tasks.

2. Foster an environment where students can discover their role within the classroom community. Often, students who feel like they don't fit in can find a sense of belonging by recognizing their importance as contributors to the larger group.

3. Pay attention to the students as they perform these tasks. These responsibilities may reveal hidden talents or weaknesses among students, providing crucial insights that enable us to offer more personalized support and guidance throughout their educational journey.

The idea behind this concept is that everyone shares responsibility for maintaining the classroom. Japan has perfected this approach, as they don't employ janitors in the same way as we do in Western countries. Instead, students in Japan are responsible for cleaning and organizing their own classrooms. While I've occasionally had my students use brooms and small vacuums in my classrooms, I've primarily taught in schools with Western-style janitorial services. However, there are various ways to involve students in taking on a small part of the responsibility for the room. Despite being labor-intensive, I've experienced significant success in ensuring that all my students have some daily or weekly role in maintaining the classroom.

One particularly positive aspect I've noticed is that not only do students feel a greater sense of responsibility themselves, but they also encourage each other to be more responsible, especially when their roles involve rectifying someone else's mess. Here's an example of some roles I've assigned and how I typically implement this.

Here's a breakdown of some of the various classroom roles and responsibilities I've employed over the years:

1. **Room Cleaners:** A group of 2 to 3 students is responsible for maintaining the cleanliness and organization of the classroom.

2. **Sweepers or Vacuumers:** 1 or 2 students are tasked with sweeping the hard floor or identifying areas that require vacuuming.

3. **Pledge Leader:** 1 student is responsible for leading the class in reciting the pledge.

4. **Materials Organizers:** 1 or more students are in charge of keeping materials organized. This can be flexible and expand to involve more students if there are multiple areas in the classroom with different materials, especially in group

workspaces.

5. **Desk and Cubby Checkers:** 1, 2, or 3 students are responsible for checking desks or cubbies and notifying their classmates if they need to tidy up. This complements some of the whole-class responsibilities practiced at the beginning of the school year. It requires practice and rehearsal.
6. **Line Leaders:** Lead the class during transitions.
7. **Line Managers:** Assist in maintaining order within the line during transitions.
8. **Door Holders:** 1 or more students are designated to hold the door open for the class.
9. **Pet Caretakers:** If there's a classroom pet, students take on the important responsibility of caring for it.
10. **Class Managers:** 1 or more students help ensure that everyone is fulfilling their assigned roles and responsibilities. You can provide them with checklists for added organization, although this may become complex depending on the number of tasks.
11. **Teacher Helper:** Assists the teacher with tasks such as passing out papers or running errands to the office.
12. **Student Medic:** Responsible for accompanying sick classmates to the nurse's office and ensuring they have their belongings if they need to go home.

These roles not only distribute responsibilities but also promote a sense of teamwork and shared accountability within the classroom.

These are just examples of roles I've used in the past. I don't assign them every year because different classrooms have varying dynamics that require different types of responsibilities. Here are a few practices I've developed over the years to enhance the effectiveness of these roles:

1. **Rotate Jobs:** At the start of the school year, I rotate the assigned roles frequently, typically on a daily or every few days basis. This way, each student has a chance to experience all the different roles. After they've had a turn at each role, they keep their assigned roles for a full week. I do this for several reasons:

   - It ensures that every student has an opportunity to try out every role, both the enjoyable ones and the less exciting ones.
   - It prevents me from consistently assigning the more challenging roles to the responsible students.
   - It allows me to gain insights into my students' abilities and traits that I might not otherwise notice.

2. **Fun Names:** Initially, I start with basic names for the roles, but I eventually turn to the students to brainstorm creative and entertaining names. This exercise provides an opportunity to discuss linguistic concepts like alliteration, onomatopoeia, and rhyming. For example, "Pet Caretaker" might transform into "PET PROTECTOR," and "Pledge Leader" could become "PLEDGE PRESIDENT." This not only makes the roles more engaging but also garners more buy-in and enthusiasm from the class.

Make It Personal

Many teachers showcase their students' work in the classroom, a practice I also embrace. However, I take it a step further by actively involving my students in decorating the room. I encourage them to share their ideas, and if a suggestion resonates with the class, we often put it to a vote to decide whether to implement it. This collaborative approach fosters a sense of community among us.

Moreover, I give students the opportunity to contribute to the classroom's décor by asking them to suggest items or even bring in their creations. Typically, this involves students drawing pictures that we proudly display on the walls. Occasionally, students have brought in decorative items. Before accepting any items from students, I always ensure to seek parental consent, and I make it clear that we won't accept anything expensive or valuable. Nevertheless, we've welcomed plants, posters, and various knickknacks that have enriched our classroom environment.

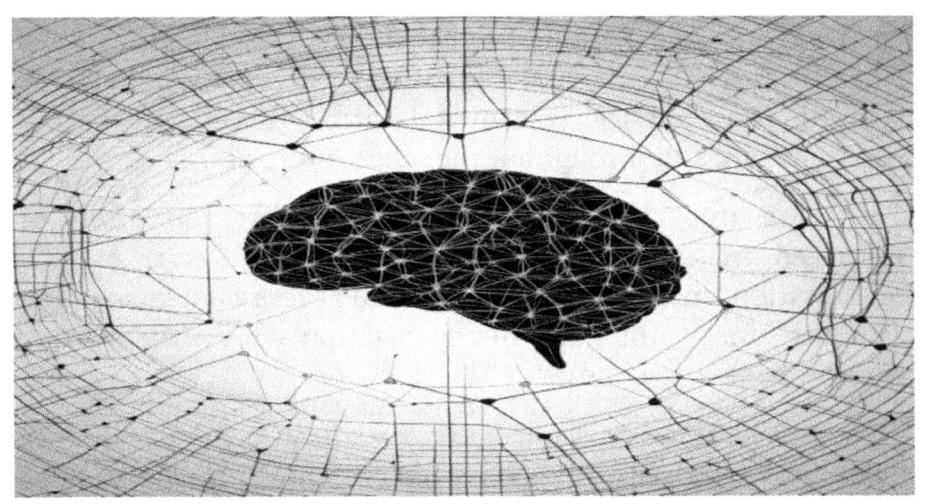

PART 7: MANAGING BEHAVIOR

Behavior management is a critical skill to develop as a teacher, but also a tricky one.　　This is tricky because there is no "one right way" to manage a classroom.　　At the same time, many schools can be overly focused on a one size fits all strategy.　　Instead of getting into a long opinionated rant on the multifaceted failings of our school system and it's ability to implement good school and classroom management,　I just want to highlight a couple areas I think are important.

A Safe Learning Environment:

First and foremost a classroom needs to be safe. Without a safe environment, effective learning becomes significantly more challenging. It's essential to take every possible measure to establish and maintain classroom safety. This involves protecting students from physical and mental harm while they are within the classroom and throughout the school premises.

There are important aspects to safety that too often get neglected in classrooms such as control, a sense of flow, organization, and consistency. Neglecting these elements can lead to chaos, uncertainty, and disorganization within the learning environment.

There's a common misconception in education that equates a quiet classroom with ineffectiveness, or that granting students more physical freedom is better. However, I believe the opposite to be true. In every setting, specific rules and behavior guidelines are essential to create a safe and effective learning environment. A classroom is a unique environment, it is a confined space with many individuals. To optimize such situations, a degree of control, a sense of flow, organization, and consistency is vital to maintain a safe atmosphere.

Noise and movement are prime examples of elements that are often overlooked or misunderstood, undermining a teacher's ability to sustain a safe classroom. Allowing excessive noise and unrestricted movement tends to lead to chaos, uncertainty, and disorganization. The reason for this neglect often stems from an oversimplification of academic practices. For instance, we can focus in on noise. The idea that children talking is beneficial for learning can lead to the misconception that a noisy classroom is always productive. This misinterpretation can result in teachers receiving negative reviews from principals because their classrooms are perceived as too quiet. These misconceptions can undermine effective teaching practices because now teachers are focused more on just having a constantly noisy environment where students are always talking and moving. What good teaching really needs though is situational balance. Some things call for different levels of noise and movement. Classrooms that don't have this balance and are always noisy hinder student success, primarily by diminishing a sense of control in the classroom which leads to a diminished sense of safety.

Finally, let me introduce a somewhat radical viewpoint. To build successful educational institutions and classrooms, our society needs to undergo a transformation. This is especially crucial in ensuring safety. In situations where a child or a parent poses any physical safety threat, it is imperative that they are not allowed to attend the school until they have clearly demonstrated rehabilitation. The same principle can apply to emotional threats to safety, although defining these threats can be more complex, and that discussion goes beyond the scope of this book.

The Complexity of Classroom Rules and the Need for Clarity:

In a classroom setting, it's vital to recognize that a mere five to ten rules won't suffice. This is because we're essentially teaching students the intricate, unspoken social and communal norms that govern our society – norms that these students might not be familiar with due to their diverse backgrounds. With a wide array of students from various backgrounds, teachers constantly encounter numerous rules and norms that require both teaching and enforcement.

For instance, let's take the broad concept of "respect." Within this concept lie countless smaller rules and procedures that students must grasp to consistently demonstrate respect throughout the day. This includes showing respect when speaking, when others are speaking, during restroom breaks, towards personal belongings, in small group interactions, and when entering or leaving the classroom, etc.… The list will go on and on.

Many students may not have had the opportunity to learn these rules, which highlights the disparity between novice and expert thinking. We too often assume that these rules and norms are already understood, but this is not the case. In fact, many students are raised in environments that endorse entirely different rules, procedures, and expectations. Thus, students need to not only learn the school's procedures, expectations, and rules but also develop the ability to "code-switch" between these and their home environment.

An argument occasionally made by teachers is that having too many rules and procedures stifles creativity, individualism, and the ability to express oneself freely. However, I disagree with this stance. Such thinking tends to define creativity and individualism narrowly. The reality is that implementing rules, expectations, and procedures in a structured manner actually provides students with more opportunities to acquire knowledge and use it creatively. Again a school is a very specific kind of environment. In this this specific environment too much individual freedom easily infringes on other's freedoms. For this environment an organized and structured approach is what contributes to educational equity.

The key balance lies in clearly understanding the rules, expectations, and procedures – their purpose and how to implement them fairly. When done correctly, with care and a genuine desire to improve students' experiences, these measures are not oppressive but rather pathways to progress and greater educational equality. Additionally, it's important to explain to students why these rules, procedures, and expectations exist.

However, I think it is important point out at this juncture that when explaining rules, procedures and expectation to students that it is an explanation, not a discussion. While discussions are valuable, they should be held at the appropriate time and place. Students, while having good ideas, may lack the comprehensive knowledge necessary to understand the reasons behind certain rules. Even if they do know the reasons they may lack the actual experience to really understand them. If students truly are passionate about it, we should provide them an appropriate opportunity to express their argument. Also, if we don't approach it this way, we open the opportunity for students who just want to argue with the teacher or throw off the class.

Of course, there are many more complexities with behavior involving parents, society, and politics in education. Nevertheless, I one things teachers should be taught in teachers college is that public education is lacking a common purpose. It cannot cater to everyone's needs and desires. Teachers and schools can take steps work to remedy this by clearly and specifically defining their purpose for education and a school's purpose, acknowledging their limitations, and moving toward a more targeted approach. It's a small step in the right direction toward improving education.

The Carrot and The Stick

Dealing with behavioral issues necessitates a balanced approach that incorporates both incentives (the "carrot") and consequences (the "stick"). The key here, as always, is finding that essential balance.

It can be frustrating to witness some schools predominantly emphasizing the positive behaviors systems and ignoring the consequences. While this approach may provide immediate feel-good results, it falls short when it's the sole focus. In reality, overemphasizing positive is neither beneficial nor successful. Life itself presents us with a mixture of positive and negative consequences for our actions, and a one-sided approach doesn't adequately prepare students for these real-life challenges.

A significant deficiency in many school behavior plans and systems is the absence of meaningful consequences for inappropriate behaviors. This gap may arise from a combination of factors, including a fear of parental reactions and a lack of alignment among schools and society regarding their shared purpose. However, I believe that these challenges should not deter us. To be clear, I am not advocating for corporal punishment; rather, I am advocating for balance, balance that encompasses both positive incentives for behavior and clear, well-defined consequences that students are expected to uphold. Unfortunately, this equilibrium is often lacking in public schools.

Having these clear goals incentives and consequence are important for teachers to be able to manage a class. When dealing with inappropriate behaviors, it is essential to respond swiftly and decisively. This should be followed by a clear explanation of what the student did wrong and why it is unacceptable behavior. Furthermore, it's crucial to provide guidance and teach alternative, appropriate behaviors for similar situations. Again we are going back to "code switching". Many times have students have been taught these behaviors at home. Students exhibit these behaviors because they are unaware of the more appropriate behavior or is just has not been enforced enough for them to know.

Again we are coming back to this disconnect between novice and expert understanding. Now it is regarding behavior. Often, we assume that students comprehend their behaviors and motivations when, in reality, they often do not. This lack of understanding is a root cause of many behavior problems. Rather than making excuses for students' actions, our focus should be on actively teaching, practicing, and encouraging the desired behaviors.

This extends beyond typical rude or hurtful behaviors; it encompasses behaviors essential for effective classroom participation and learning. For instance, consider a student who fidgets excessively and disrupts the class. Simply providing them with a fidget toy or a special seat is rarely sufficient and can sometimes lead to more distractions. Also it is not teaching or enforcing any expected behaviors which is always what we should try first. What we need is a multi-faceted approach.

First, clarity is vital. We must explain what constitutes good learning behavior and why it's important. For example, we can convey that sitting still allows better focus on content and reduces distractions for oneself and others. Many students may not have received this guidance before. We also need to be clear and say that this is the general expectation for students.

Enforcing these expectations involves utilizing both rewards and consequences. When a student displays disruptive behavior, it's essential to respond swiftly and with clear correction. This correction should be delivered in a firm yet neutral tone, avoiding yelling or unkindness. Actions like temporarily removing the disruptive object or relocating it may be necessary. Immediately following this correction, it's important to offer specific feedback on how to prevent such behavior in the future. For instance, you can say something like, "You tend to play with things in your hand, so during the lesson, try to keep your hands free from objects."

To maintain this balance, it's crucial to actively identify and commend students when they exhibit appropriate behavior. There's no one-size-fits-all process for this; it's a matter of combining the two essential components. To make this approach effective, teachers must consistently be alert to opportunities where students demonstrate the desired behavior. In many instances, teachers may even need to take an extra step and create scenarios that allow students to display appropriate behavior, especially at the beginning of the school year. As we provide clear positive reinforcement, our particular focus should be on students who have previously faced reprimands.

Recognizing Small Achievements

It's crucial that we take the time to celebrate these small achievements in our students. Don't hesitate to offer small rewards like stickers or candy. While our ultimate aim is for students to exhibit desirable behavior without the need for rewards, this transformation can be a long and sometimes challenging journey. Striving for a balance between rewards and intrinsic motivation is often effective in most situations.

Moreover, I firmly believe that stickers and candy can be effective incentives for individuals of all ages. I recall one of my favorite high school teachers who would stroll down the hallways, distributing Jolly Ranchers along with compliments or sharing a funny joke. This simple act of rewarding and encouraging students made him one of the most popular teachers. He remains strong in my memory almost 30 years later. It's a testament to how small gestures can significantly influence students' behavior and attitudes. Even as adults, we frequently engage in similar practices, using food, coffee, and other treats as tokens of encouragement and camaraderie; it's a human thing.

Addressing Criticism

It's important to acknowledge that this approach is not without its critics, and addressing these concerns is essential. One common criticism revolves around the belief that this approach may be too harsh or inappropriate, especially when dealing with students who may have underlying conditions like ADHD or dyslexia. Some teachers argue that enforcing consequences for these students may seem unfair, as these behaviors are not entirely within their control.

However, the reality is quite the opposite. It's unfair not to hold these students accountable for their actions, or to allow their diagnoses to serve as excuses for their behavior. Most of the time, a diagnosis doesn't alter the fundamental need for guidance and support. In fact, that need remains the same, and at times, it might even be more significant.

Consider a student diagnosed with ADHD who struggles with

excessive fidgeting. Regardless of the diagnosis, the ultimate goal remains consistent: to teach, encourage, and hopefully assist the student in gaining control over their body and actions.

My understanding of this approach has developed not only through my experiences but also through self-education in fields such as child development and developmental psychology. I don't claim to be an expert; instead, I strive to apply the knowledge I gather from experts to my classroom practices. In addition to this, I have personally achieved significant success using this approach throughout most of my teaching career. I arrived at this understanding early on and have consistently seen positive results not only in my own classroom but also in other teachers known for consistently outstanding classes.

With 23 years of experience, I have consistently found that this approach works more often than not, resulting in consistently excellent classes year after year with minimal to no behavior issues. My students consistently express their appreciation for my class and me as a teacher. Parents consistently provide me with high reviews, and my students consistently demonstrate strong academic growth. In contrast, I have noted that teachers take a counter view, often are the ones who encounter recurring behavior problems year after year, along with a multitude of excuses for why these issues occur.

Ultimately, our goal is to help students grow into independent learners who can participate effectively in society as adults. To achieve this, we must assist them in gaining control over their impulses, honing their focus, and developing self-regulation skills. This includes teaching techniques to manage movements, calm their minds and bodies, and enhance their ability to sustain attention—all essential aspects of effective learning.

Addressing Educational Needs

One recurring observation I've made year after year is that some children tend to misbehave during specific periods, often coinciding with particular subjects or types of work. Upon closer examination, it becomes apparent that their misbehavior usually stems from the fact that the assigned tasks are either too easy or too challenging for them.

To illustrate this, consider my role as a third-grade teacher. Each year, I encounter students who struggle with writing, and many of them exhibit behavioral issues. To address this, I take the time to ensure these students receive focused instruction on writing skills, aiming to help them become proficient writers. This involves working on their penmanship, guiding them in forming letters, and encouraging daily writing practice. This straightforward approach consistently results in happy and proud students who gain the confidence to progress to the next grade. Moreover, as any educator knows, the ability to write with fluency, endurance, and clarity positively influences all other aspects of learning, enhancing the overall educational experience for the child.

We need to ensure that all students master certain foundational skills, which are crucial for effective communication and overall progress. These fundamental skills include speaking, reading, writing, basic math and number sense, as well as self-control, especially in terms of students' ability to focus and work for extended periods.

For instance, when students find the material too easy and require a challenge, a two-pronged approach is necessary. Firstly, students often need their perception of their own knowledge to be challenged. They may have a lot of experience in a particular area and believe they know more than they actually do. While it might be challenging for students to accept this, assessments and tests can help dispel this illusion. Many times, this approach resolves the issue, as students realize they don't know everything and redirect their energy towards learning what they need to know.

However, there are cases where students genuinely grasp the content and need to be pushed further. This doesn't necessarily involve extending the same activity; instead, it often means providing opportunities for these students to delve deeper into the subject matter. Failing to offer such opportunities not only hinders individual progress but also leads to disengagement and behavioral problems in students who are not sufficiently challenged.

It might seem like common sense to address students' needs where they are, but year after year, in every school I've worked in, I encounter students falling into one of the two categories mentioned earlier. Somehow they passed through several grades without their deficits being addressed properly. In each case, I concentrate on identifying their deficiencies and then provide encouragement, pushing them to excel, offering assistance, and, most importantly, make sure they see their growth and success in those areas. As a result, their behavioral issues gradually disappear, they start enjoying school more, and their confidence in their ability to learn improves. I can't pinpoint the exact barrier, but I am convinced that students would benefit significantly if we put more effort into actively addressing their individual needs.

Happiness:

Happiness is one of those weird things I have always been interested in. So it makes sense that it is something I have paid attention to in my learning endeavors. It is also something that I have spent a lot of time thinking about in the classroom.

Happiness is a complicated and diverse emotional state. While happiness is a broad term there is a lot of science out there that can help us understand what make us happy. We can use some of that science to help us as teacher in the classroom.

Neurotransmitters

Neurotransmitters are chemical messengers that facilitate communication between nerve cells (neurons) in the nervous system, enabling the transmission of information throughout the body.

To cultivate a happy school environment, it's crucial to engage in activities that promote the production of these neurotransmitters. What often is ignored in schools is the identification of behaviors that stimulate the release of these chemicals and utilizing them to our advantage. In fact, schools sometimes inadvertently inhibit the release of these neurotransmitters.

The challenge arises when we incorrectly associate happiness with obtaining all our desires, which can lead to unhappiness and even depression. Students who get to have breaks whenever they want. Students who don't have expectations to behave or do any work. Students who are never pushed. These don't really promote happiness, in fact they will create downward spirals of depression and lack of purpose that may be difficult to get out of later in life. Genuine student happiness in school is rooted in a secure and balanced environment where they can face challenges and achieve success. It entails nurturing camaraderie, purpose, and a sense of accomplishment through hard work.

By incorporating activities in school that boost the output of these chemicals, we can contribute to a happier environment. What tends to be overlooked in schools is the understanding of which behaviors trigger these chemicals and how to encourage them.

Serotonin and Dopamine: This is a huge one. These are chemicals that keeps us addicted to our phones and makes video games so powerful. They are triggered when we achieve small accomplishments. They can be addictive, but also we can harness this addictive power for learning. As I said before we are learning from the power success of video games.

In school we need to provide lots of small successful moments for students. Each moment will provide a boost of Dopamine. This works for behavior and academics both. This is why I say that at first, you may need to manufacture moments of success to get students started. We need to challenge students regularly and have them pursue goals. As we are doing this we are instilling a senses of meaning and accomplishment. Students need to hear " You Did It!" Or to say, "I Did It!". After some initial success this will create a feedback loop that will reinforce the positive behaviors and build self-esteem. It will make student more confident in what they do and increase their future success.

I can't stress enough that at the beginning this is hard. Where we tend to go wrong in schools is that we don't push kids to do hard things. So often students come to me and they can't read or do basic math facts. This is because no one ever pushed them before. They just let them off with excuses. Once they get to me, I make them do it. They don't like it at first, but I explain that the expectation is that they try and work at it in my class. I encourage them support them and help them in this endeavor. I get family involved when I can. I manufacture successful events, but keep pushing consistently. In every case these students improve in the academic skill, and in their attitude towards that skill.

Serotonin and Endorphins: Give students breaks and get them outside for recess. These chemicals are released during periods of relaxation and exercise. Providing a balance of both during the day will increase the production of these chemicals.

Oxytocin: When we establish a safe, caring, and nurturing environment, we promote the release of oxytocin. It's also crucial to create situations where students can work together productively and supportively.

I continue to believe that attaining happiness in school is a straightforward goal. The challenge frequently emerges when we incorrectly link happiness with obtaining all our desires, which can actually result in the opposite – unhappiness and even depression. Genuine student happiness in school is rooted in a secure and balanced environment, where they can gain valuable experiences by conquering challenges and achieving success. It involves fostering a sense of camaraderie, purpose, and accomplishment through diligent effort.

Embrace Weird:

Students and kids display a unique and captivating quality. They are weird. They are drawn to wonder, engage in flights of fancy, and are deeply fascinated by things that ignite their imagination. As they mature, they embark on a journey to comprehend the world, uncover their identities, and establish their roles within it. This process evolves in parallel with the ongoing development of their brains, encouraging them to take risks, nurture their curiosity, and question everything. All of this transpires while they remain relatively inexperienced about the world, lacking the life knowledge to guide them.

Effective teachers embrace students' curiosity, allowing them to explore their imaginations and adapt to contemporary trends, all while keeping them grounded in reality and ensuring they don't stray too far. They strike a balance between the excitement of the new and the practicality of knowledge and learning. By doing so, teachers position themselves as reliable and trustworthy figures in their students' lives. This fosters a sense of safety and security, enabling students to confide in them.

Play and hang out:

If you're going to be a teacher, it's crucial to actively participate in their world. Join them during recess, take part in their activities, and engage with them. For older students, spend time with them in the hallways, have lunch together, and establish clear boundaries, especially for the older age group. I'll be honest; this can be a bit challenging as students grow older, but doing what you can is important and it can have a significant impact.

In fact one aspect that might be overlooked here is that setting boundaries is a valuable life lesson that teaches about different types of relationships and how to navigate them in life. Teachers must serve as role models and mentors for students, particularly as they enter their teenage years. This is a critical stage of development where adolescents start seeking guidance beyond their families, looking to others to learn about the world around them. It's during this period that we must provide students with positive adult role models to help them navigate the broader world effectively.

PART 8: HOMEWORK

Should students be assigned homework or not? I encourage all teachers, students and parents to take time and look deeply into this topic on their own. You'll likely discover numerous perspectives and opinions, but there's a subtle thread of consistency that underlies this issue.

Much like testing, homework can be a valuable and potent tool for teaching and learning. I would even argue that it is necessary. However, when executed poorly, it can have detrimental effects on students' emotions, motivation, and perception of the learning process. In the following discussion, I aim to leverage the information I've already shared to analyze the pros and cons of homework. This way, individuals can make more informed decisions regarding whether or not to assign homework.

I want to be clear from the start: I am in favor of homework at every age, but I fully comprehend the arguments against it.

I believe that if homework is not going to be administered in a well-thought-out manner, it might be preferable not to assign any homework at all. But when done in a thoughtful and supportive way, it can have dramatic impacts on student achievement in the long run.

Homework offers two remarkable benefits. Firstly, it naturally incorporates retrieval and spacing into the learning process. Secondly, it diversifies the environments in which students must recall information. As previously discussed, this is crucial for fostering broader connections, enhancing retrieval strength, and strengthening storage strength in memory. Homework presents educators with an incredible opportunity to expand and reinforce learning.

The complexity of homework arises from the fact that it demands a specific level of environmental control, self-discipline, motivation, planning, time management, and self-confidence from the students. Unfortunately, many students and parents struggle with these aspects, and this is where the entire process can easily unravel.

Considering all these factors, we must exercise caution in the type and manner of homework assignments we provide. In most cases, homework should be manageable for students. Assignments that are overly challenging or time-consuming can erode a student's confidence, motivation, and foster negative feelings towards learning. When homework becomes excessively difficult or demanding, and there is a lack of support either from the teacher or at home, it can lead to power struggles between parents and students, teachers and students, and even teachers and parents. This toxic atmosphere can seriously disrupt a student's emotional well-being, motivation, and self-assurance.

These are the primary factors highlighted in homework studies that demonstrate its ineffectiveness. These studies suggest that the emotional toll and negative outcomes associated with homework outweigh the benefits it may offer.

Another issue with homework is that it can sometimes lose its meaningful purpose and devolve into mere "busywork." Many assignments teachers give end up feeling like tedious chores rather than serving as valuable retrieval practice or constructive experiences that enrich learning. In my view, this boils down to the perspectives on homework, its purpose, the amount assigned, and its duration. Striking the right balance among these factors can mean the difference between busywork and a useful homework assignment.

On the flip side, when we provide assignments that are more thoughtful and less burdensome, especially when aiming to boost students' confidence and motivation, we open up significant opportunities to enhance their self-assurance, motivation, and overall positive attitudes towards learning. Moreover, we can empower students to become more self-reliant learners, which is a primary goal. This ideal balance lies within the concept of "desirable difficulties." It involves finding tasks that require just enough effort, not too much, to be attainable. When students complete such tasks, their brains release rewarding chemicals that reinforce their sense of accomplishment. This mechanism mirrors why video games are both popular and effective; they have essentially mastered the concept of "desirable difficulties" by providing gradually increasing levels of challenge and ample opportunities for success.

The ultimate goal would be to replicate this concept in homework and, ideally, in all school assignments. This is precisely what you'll find in studies that demonstrate the potential effectiveness of homework when it aligns with the principle of "desirable difficulties.

Feedback plays a crucial role in the effectiveness of homework. Without feedback, homework may not reach its full potential. In this context, I firmly believe that more immediate feedback yields better results. It's important to note that providing feedback doesn't have to be time-consuming. A quick review of answers as a whole class, where students can check their work themselves, can be quite efficient. Especially in the context of homework and motivation, students need to understand that what they do at home is significant, connected to their school learning, and relevant to their overall education. Feedback helps establish this connection while also offering opportunities for assessment and reflection.

However, the origins of this issue can be traced back to the classroom. Teachers need to have a deeper understanding of their students' abilities. It's crucial to know what students comprehend and where they might struggle before assigning homework. Homework should primarily serve as a retrieval event for information that students have already successfully engaged with in class, not as a way to introduce entirely new concepts. Unfortunately, this isn't always the case. Returning to the topic of assessment, we often fall short in this area. Our educational goals and standards can be vague and broad. Our assessments may be poorly aligned with student learning or too infrequent. Our teaching methods might not align with the questions we ask. Too often, we find ourselves following a curriculum we didn't design, teaching lessons we didn't create or vet, and assigning work that isn't well-matched to what we've taught. Consequently, when students receive a score like 5 out of 10, teachers might simply categorize it as "approaching" without delving deeper into the learning process.

One significant challenge that teachers frequently encounter is being constrained by a rigid educational path that doesn't allow much room for flexibility. We're often told to move from point A to point B within a specified timeframe, with little opportunity for deviation. Consequently, teachers can find themselves drifting away from the core principles of teaching and learning, instead becoming facilitators of lessons.

This issue becomes increasingly daunting as students progress through their education, resulting in a widening knowledge gap among them. Assigning homework to a class where reading abilities span multiple grade levels, from several grades above to several grades below, presents a perplexing dilemma. Unfortunately, there's no straightforward solution to this problem. While we can employ various strategies such as adapting the assignments, providing scaffolded supports, or offering after-school assistance, these measures often fall short of completely bridging the knowledge gap. In attempting to help "some" of the students, teachers frequently exhaust themselves, sometimes at the expense of their emotional well-being.

I, too, am subject to the limitations of this system. I don't claim to possess all the answers, but I offer advice based on what I have found to be effective and work toward continuous improvement.

As an elementary teacher, I don't assign homework every day. Instead, I've found success in a different approach. At the start of the week, I provide students with assignments and inform them that they have the entire week to complete it. I encourage them to tackle it as soon as possible and discourage procrastination. To reinforce this, I follow up daily, reminding them to seek assistance if needed. These assignments are typically ones I'm confident most students understand. At the beginning of the school year, I keep them short and straightforward.

I also prioritize communication with parents and strive to establish positive home-school connections. I send advice to parents on how they can support their children with homework and explain why I consider it important. I even share concepts like retrieval practice and spacing with them. When students return completed assignments, I celebrate their accomplishment to boost their sense of pride.

As the school year progresses and I observe students consistently engaging with homework, I may introduce more challenging assignments or gradually increase the complexity or time required for the work. However, I always remain attuned to the students' response. If too many students struggle or are unable to complete the work, I scale back the assignments. Additionally, I offer strong support to students who find the homework challenging. While I encourage them to complete the work, I also extend grace if they cannot. I make it a point to assist those who seek extra help.

To maximize the benefits of homework, consider the following key principles:

1. **Consistency:** Maintain a consistent schedule for assigning and completing homework.
2. **Home/School Connection:** Foster a strong connection between home and school by communicating with parents about the importance of homework and ways they can support their child's learning.
3. **Quiet, Independent Workspace:** Encourage students to have a dedicated, quiet, and independent space for doing their homework, minimizing distractions as much as possible.
4. **Distraction Management:** Advise parents and students to reduce distractions during homework time to the extent feasible.
5. **Appropriate Challenge:** Provide assignments that are easily manageable to set students up for success.
6. **Emphasize Importance:** Stress the significance of homework in facilitating learning and personal development.
7. **Grace and Patience:** Show understanding and patience for incomplete homework while maintaining a balanced approach with positive and negative consequences.
8. **Frequent Rewards:** Offer regular rewards and celebrate accomplishments, especially for students who may struggle with homework.

By following these principles, you can enhance the effectiveness of homework and create a supportive learning environment for students.

PART 9: MUSIC AND LEARNING

Is it appropriate to play music in the classroom? I'm a strong advocate for incorporating music into the classroom, but not all the time. The question isn't whether to play music or not, but rather when is it suitable and what type of music should be played?

The most straightforward way to address this question is by considering working memory. Music represents another stream of information entering working memory. However, it occupies a significant amount of space, which can pose an issue if students are engaged in tasks that demand their full attention.

Therefore, if I have students working on tasks that require deep focus, undivided attention, or they are facing challenges, my answer is no, I don't play music. This is because music consumes valuable working memory capacity that they need to process other critical information.

What about times when focus is less of an issue? Are there benefits to music?

Mozart Effect:

In short, The Mozart Effect isn't a real phenomenon.

The "Mozart Effect" is a term often used to describe the popular belief that listening to the music of Wolfgang Amadeus Mozart or other classical compositions can enhance cognitive abilities. This idea gained considerable attention following a study conducted by researchers Frances Rauscher, Gordon Shaw, and Katherine Ky in 1993. However, it's worth noting that the findings of this study were likely exaggerated and may have been more attributable to individual differences in student performance. Moreover, attempts to replicate the study have not been successful.

The impact of music on learning is a complex topic, with both positive and negative effects influenced by factors such as the type of music, the learning context, and individual preferences. Many of the positive benefits associated with music are linked to its context-dependent aspects when used as a study aid.

This means that if you listen to music while learning and then listen to the same music when attempting to recall the information, the music can serve as a memory cue for that information. The repetitive or rhythmic patterns in music can aid in memory retention. For many people, associating information with a melody or rhythm makes it easier to remember. Similar principles apply to actions like chewing bubble gum or studying in a specific room. Ultimately, it's about the memory cues created by your external environment that connect to the information you're learning. Remember, learning occurs in tandem with the environment around us, including sounds, smells, and tastes. Our brain's central executive system decides what to focus on and what to disregard.

While this can be a valuable tool in certain situations, it's important to recognize that we may not always have the same environment or the ability to play music when we need to recall information, such as in a school setting. Additionally, if the goal is to establish a robust retrieval memory, we aim for the information to be "context independent" rather than "context dependent," meaning we want to be able to recall it in various environments, not just one.

Beyond the cognitive effects, there are emotional dimensions to consider when it comes to the impact of music on learning. Music has the potential to influence our emotions, either enhancing or detracting from our overall mood, and this emotional aspect can significantly affect our comfort level and learning experience.

For instance, when we listen to upbeat and energetic music, it often has the power to boost our mood, increase motivation, and make learning activities more enjoyable. It can act as a powerful motivator, helping students remain focused and energized during tasks that might otherwise seem dull or monotonous. The right music can provide that extra push to stay engaged and enthusiastic.

Conversely, music can also easily become a distraction. In fact music is really always a distraction to some degree, but in this case we are saying is becomes a major distraction. Sometimes, the allure of the music itself can be so captivating that it hinders our ability to concentrate on the task at hand. When the music becomes the center of attention rather than a supportive backdrop, it can disrupt our focus and reduce productivity.

Furthermore, the choice of music genre can evoke various emotional responses. Certain types of music may have a calming, soothing effect, while others may evoke feelings of sadness or melancholy. These emotional responses can have a direct impact on the learning experience. For example, music that induces sadness might have a counterproductive effect on learning, impairing concentration and engagement.

Therefore, the selection of music in the learning environment should be thoughtful, taking into account both the cognitive and emotional aspects to create an atmosphere conducive to effective learning.

Music can also plan and important role in creativity and problem-solving, akin to the principles of mind-wandering and the cultivation of a positive emotional state. Much like mind-wandering, the role of music in enhancing these cognitive processes can be explained through the concept of cognitive flexibility.

Consider this scenario: When we find ourselves in a comfortable and low-pressure state, we're more likely to allow our focus to wander. In this state, we still allocate part of our working memory to the task at hand, but not its entirety. The remaining cognitive resources are left free to respond to environmental cues and stimuli. This mental flexibility creates the ideal conditions for various cognitive schemas within our brain to be activated and connected.

Music, particularly instrumental and non-distracting genres, can play a significant role in this process. Such music acts as a pleasant backdrop that enhances cognitive flexibility without overwhelming the cognitive processes necessary for the task at hand. It creates an environment in which the mind can subtly shift between the task and other elements in the surroundings.

This subtle shift allows for the activation of diverse cognitive pathways and connections that might have otherwise remained dormant. As a result, music can stimulate creative thinking and problem-solving skills by encouraging the exploration of unconventional ideas and fostering an environment where the mind is open to forming new connections and insights.

In essence, music can act as a cognitive enhancer, nurturing a state of mind conducive to creativity and problem-solving, much like the benefits gained from allowing the mind to wander in a comfortable and positive emotional state.

The big take away is that music can have both positive and negative effects. You decision to use music should involve you thinking about two things:
1. What is your purpose for the use of music.
2. What is the task you are hoping to accomplish.

Keeping in mind that the impact of music on learning varies from person to person and depends on factors like the type of music, the nature of the learning task, and individual preferences. The bottom line is music will always distract a student in some way. If you want an environment that is primed for focus, then music should not be used. The more there is to music the more distraction there is (lyrics, varied rhythm, changes to the song, etc..). At the same time, the distraction and emotional influence can lead to positive effects as well. It all boils down to the person and the situation.

In my classroom, I often incorporate music strategically to create a conducive learning environment. Here's how I typically use music:

1. **Morning Ambiance:** To start the day, I play relaxing music as students arrive. I often accompany this with videos featuring serene natural environments, underwater scenes, or animals. The primary aim here is to establish a calm and soothing atmosphere for students as they begin their day.

2. **Transition Times:** During longer transitions between activities, I occasionally use music along with a timer. Some timers have music cues associated with them. Students become accustomed to these musical cues and can gauge how much time remains based on the music. This helps maintain a sense of structure and predictability.

3. **In-Class Use:** I rarely use music during regular

class activities unless it directly complements the task. For instance, if students are engaged in activities involving cutting or preparation, I might play music to enhance the experience.

4. **Free Time:** During more relaxed or free periods, I may introduce slightly more upbeat and enjoyable music. However, I'm mindful of the fact that some students may struggle to shift their attention back and forth, so I provide reminders as needed.

Here's a summarized list of the positive and negative effects of using music in the classroom:

Positive Effects:

- **Mood Enhancement:** Pleasant and calming music can positively influence emotions and mood, creating an environment conducive to concentration and engagement.
- **Motivation and Engagement:** Upbeat and energetic music can boost motivation and make learning activities more enjoyable, helping students stay focused.
- **Memory Enhancement:** Music with repetitive patterns can aid memory retention, making it easier for students to remember information.
- **Creativity and Problem Solving:** Certain types of non-distracting music, especially instrumental genres, can stimulate creative thinking and problem-solving skills without overwhelming cognitive processes.
- **Reduced Anxiety:** Calming music can reduce anxiety and stress levels, promoting concentration and better performance under pressure.

Negative Effects:

- **Distraction:** Music, especially with lyrics or complex structures, can be distracting, competing for cognitive resources needed for learning tasks.

- **Interference with Reading and Comprehension:** Complex music with lyrics may interfere with reading comprehension, as the brain processes both written words and auditory input simultaneously.
- **Misattribution of Focus:** Multitasking with music may lead to reduced performance in both learning and music listening, as the brain's processing capacity is limited.
- **Incompatibility with Task Type:** The appropriateness of music varies with task types; it may suit repetitive tasks but hinder deep analytical thinking.
- **Individual Differences:** Preferences and sensitivities to music vary among individuals, so what aids concentration for one person may be distracting for another.

By carefully considering these factors, I aim to harness the positive effects of music while minimizing potential distractions in the classroom.

CONTINUING EDUCATION / FACT CHECKING

Like I said, I strongly encourage everyone to do more research on their own. Don't take my word for it, but find your own knowledge and your own path. This book is a culmination of knowledge that I have gained that has worked well for me in the classroom. Just remember, it is not about finding one book or one study that verifies your belief, but you need to find a body of agreed upon knowledge by experts in the field.

The following are great resources you can go to in order to find more information about the ideas I put in this book.

FREE RESOURCES PRODUCED BY EXPERTS ON THE CURRENT BODY OF THE SCIENCE OF LEARNING

Deans for Impact: The Science of Learning
https://deansforimpact.org/resources/the-science-of-learning/

The Science of Learning summarizes existing cognitive-science research on how students learn, and connects it to practical implications for teaching. The report is a resource for teacher-educators, new teachers, and anyone in the education profession who is interested in how learning takes place.
Deans for Impact believes all teacher-candidates should know the cognitive-science principles explored in The Science of Learning. And all educators, including new teachers, should be able to connect those principles to their practical implications for the classroom.

In Their Own Words: What Scholars and Teachers Want You To Know About Why and How to Apply the Science of Learning in Your Academic Setting.
By. The Society for Teaching of Psychology
https://teachpsych.org/ebooks/itow

Over the past several decades, there has been a continually growing body of scholarship focusing on conditions that promote students 'learning, retention, and transfer of academic knowledge. The term 'science of learning' is often used to describe this field of specialization. The present work is organized into five sections containing chapters focused on the history, principles, applications, and practice of the 'science of learning.'

Deans for Impact: Resources Page
https://deansforimpact.org/resources/

National Academies: Science, Engineering, Medicine: How People Learn 2
https://nap.nationalacademies.org/catalog/24783/how-people-learn-ii-learners-contexts-and-cultures

There are many reasons to be curious about the way people learn, and the past several decades have seen an explosion of research that has important implications for individual learning, schooling, workforce training, and policy.

In 2000, How People Learn: Brain, Mind, Experience, and School: Expanded Edition was published and its influence has been wide and deep. The report summarized insights on the nature of learning in school-aged children; described principles for the design of effective learning environments; and provided examples of how that could be implemented in the classroom.

Since then, researchers have continued to investigate the nature of learning and have generated new findings related to the neurological processes involved in learning, individual and cultural variability related to learning, and educational technologies. In addition to expanding scientific understanding of the mechanisms of learning and how the brain adapts throughout the lifespan, there have been important discoveries about influences on learning, particularly sociocultural factors and the structure of learning environments.

How People Learn II: Learners, Contexts, and Cultures provides a much-needed update incorporating insights gained from this research over the past decade. The book expands on the foundation laid out in the 2000 report and takes an in-depth look at the constellation of influences that affect individual learning. How People Learn II will become an indispensable resource to understand learning throughout the lifespan for educators of students and adults.

The Sutton Trust: What Makes Great Teaching.
https://www.suttontrust.com/our-research/great-teaching/

This report reviews over 200 pieces of research to identify the elements of teaching with the strongest evidence of improving attainment. It finds some common practices can be harmful to learning and have no grounding in research. Specific practices which are supported by good evidence of their effectiveness are also examined and six key factors that contribute to great teaching are identified. The report also analyses different methods of evaluating teaching including: using 'value-added' results from student test scores; observing classroom teaching; and getting students to rate the quality of their teaching.

BOOKS

How Learning Happens: Seminal Works in Educational Psychology and What They Mean in Practice
By Paul A. Kirschner, Carl Hendrick

How Learning Happens introduces 28 giants of educational research and their findings on how we learn and what we need to learn effectively, efficiently, and enjoyably. Many of these works have inspired researchers and teachers all around the world and have left a mark on how we teach today.

Exploring 28 key works on learning and teaching, chosen from the fields of educational psychology and cognitive psychology, the book offers a roadmap of the most important discoveries in how learning happens. Each chapter examines a different work and explains its significance before describing the research, its implications for practice, how it can be used in the classroom and the key takeaways for teachers. Clearly divided into six sections, the book covers:

- How the brain works and what this means for learning and teaching
- Prerequisites for learning
- How learning can be supported
- Teacher activities
- Learning in context
- Cautionary tales and the ten deadly sins of education.

Written by two leading experts and illustrated by Oliver Caviglioli, this is essential reading for teachers wanting to fully engage with and understand educational research as well as undergraduate students in the fields of education, educational psychology and the learning sciences.

How Teaching Happens: Seminal Works in Teaching and Teacher Effectiveness and What They Mean in Practice
ByPaul Kirschner, Carl Hendrick, Jim Heal

Building on their bestselling book How Learning Happens, Paul A. Kirschner and Carl Hendrick are joined by Jim Heal to explore how teaching happens. The book seeks to closely examine what makes for effective teaching in the classroom and how research on expert teaching can be used in practice.

Introducing 30 seminal works from the field of education psychology research, the learning sciences, and teaching effectiveness studies, each chapter takes an important work and illustrates clearly and concisely what the research means and how it can be used in daily practice. Divided into six sections the book covers:

- Teacher Effectiveness, Development, and Growth
- Curriculum Development / Instructional Design
- Teaching Techniques
- Pedagogical Content Knowledge
- In the Classroom
- Assessment

The book ends with a final chapter on "What's Missing?" in how teachers learn to teach.

Written by three leading experts in the field with illustrations by Oliver Cavigioli, How Teaching Happens provides a clear roadmap for classroom teachers, school leaders, and teacher trainers/trainees on what effective teaching looks like in practice.

Make It Stick: The Science of Successful Learning
By: Peter C. Brown

Tales of incidents in the lives of real people illuminate what the latest science tells us about how learning and memory work.

Drawing on recent discoveries in cognitive psychology and other disciplines, Make It Stick turns conventional wisdom on its head, entertains, and offers practical tips to all who are interested in the challenge of lifelong growth and self-improvement.

Why Don't Students Like School? A Cognitive Scientist Answers Questions About How the Mind Works and What It Means for the Classroom
By: Daniel T. Willingham

Kids are naturally curious, but when it comes to school, it seems like their minds are turned off. Why is it that they can remember the smallest details from their favorite television programs, yet miss the most obvious questions on their history test? Cognitive scientist Dan Willingham has focused his acclaimed research on the biological and cognitive basis of learning and has a deep understanding of the daily challenges faced by classroom teachers. This book will help teachers improve their practice by explaining how they and their students think and learn - revealing the importance of story, emotion, memory, context, and routine in building knowledge and creating lasting learning experiences.

Teaching Minds: How Cognitive Science Can Save Our Schools
By: Roger Schank

From grade school to graduate school, from the poorest public institutions to the most affluent private ones, our educational system is failing students. In his provocative new book, cognitive scientist and best-selling author Roger Schank argues that class size, lack of parental involvement, and other commonly cited factors have nothing to do with why students are not learning. The culprit is a system of subject-based instruction and the solution is cognitive-based learning. This groundbreaking book defines what it would mean to teach thinking. The time is now for schools to start teaching minds!

How We Learn: The Surprising Truth About When, Where, and Why It Happens By: Benedict Carey

In the tradition of The Power of Habit and Thinking, Fast and Slow comes a practical, playful, and endlessly fascinating guide to what we really know about learning and memory today - and how we can apply it to our own lives.From an early age, it is drilled into our heads: Restlessness, distraction, and ignorance are the enemies of success. We're told that learning is all self-discipline, that we must confine ourselves to designated study areas, turn off the music, and maintain a strict ritual if we want to ace that test, memorize that presentation, or nail that piano recital.But what if almost everything we were told about learning is wrong? And what if there was a way to achieve more with less effort?

When Can You Trust the Experts? How to Tell Good Science from Bad in Education
by Daniel T. Willingham

Clear, easy principles to spot what's nonsense and what's reliable Each year, teachers, administrators, and parents face a barrage of new education software, games, workbooks, and professional development programs purporting to be "based on the latest research." While some of these products are rooted in solid science, the research behind many others is grossly exaggerated. This new book, written by a top thought leader, helps everyday teachers, administrators, and family members - who don't have years of statistics courses under their belts - separate the wheat from the chaff and determine which new educational approaches are scientifically supported and worth adopting.

Understanding How We Learn: A Visual Guide
by Yana Weinstein and Megan Sumeracki

Educational practice does not, for the most part, rely on research findings. Instead, there's a preference for relying on our intuitions about what's best for learning. But relying on intuition may be a bad idea for teachers and learners alike.This accessible guide helps teachers to integrate effective, research-backed strategies for learning into their classroom practice. The book explores exactly what constitutes good evidence for effective learning and teaching strategies, how to make evidence-based judgments instead of relying on intuition, and how to apply findings from cognitive psychology directly to the classroom.Including real-life examples and case studies, FAQs, and a wealth of engaging illustrations to explain complex concepts and emphasize key points, the book is divided into four parts:Evidence-based education and the science of learning Basics of human cognitive processes Strategies for effective learning Tips for students, teachers, and parent Written by "The Learning Scientists" and fully illustrated by Oliver Caviglioli, Understanding How We Learn is a rejuvenating and fresh examination of cognitive psychology's application to education. This is an essential read for all teachers and educational practitioners, designed to convey the concepts of research to the reality of a teacher's classroom.

Seven Myths About Education
by Daisy Christodoulou

In this controversial new book, Daisy Christodoulou offers a thought-provoking critique of educational orthodoxy. Drawing on her recent experience of teaching in challenging schools, she shows through a wide range of examples and case studies just how much classroom practice contradicts basic scientific principles. She examines seven widely-held beliefs which are holding back pupils and teachers:
- Facts prevent understanding
- Teacher-led instruction is passive
- The 21st century fundamentally changes everything
- You can always just look it up
- We should teach transferable skills
- Projects and activities are the best way to learn
- Teaching knowledge is indoctrination.

In each accessible and engaging chapter, Christodoulou sets out the theory of each myth, considers its practical implications and shows the worrying prevalence of such practice. Then, she explains exactly why it is a myth, with reference to the principles of modern cognitive science. She builds a powerful case explaining how governments and educational organisations around the world have let down teachers and pupils by promoting and even mandating evidence-less theory and bad practice.This blisteringly incisive and urgent text is essential reading for all teachers, teacher training students, policy makers, head teachers, researchers and academics around the world.

What Every Teacher Needs to Know About Psychology
by David Didau and Nick Rose

Much of what we do in classrooms is intuitive, steered by what 'feels right', but all too often intuition proves a poor, sometimes treacherous guide. Although what we know about the workings of the human brain is still pitifully little, the science of psychology can and has revealed certain surprising findings that teachers would do well to heed. Over the past few decades, psychological research has made real strides into understanding how we learn, but it's only in the last few years that education has become aware of these insights. Part of the problem is a tendency amongst teachers to resist being told 'what works' if it conflicts with intuition. Whilst we cannot and should not relinquish our professional judgement in the face of outlandish claims, we should at least be aware of what scientists have discovered about learning, thinking, motivation, behaviour and assessment over the past few decades. This though is far easier said than done. Every year thousands of research papers are published, some of which contradict each other. How can busy teachers know which research is worth investing time in reading and understanding? Here, David Didau and Nick Rose attempt to lay out the evidence and theoretical perspectives on what we believe are the most important and useful psychological principles of which teacher ought to be aware. That is not to say this book contains everything you might ever need to know - there is no way it could - it is merely a primer. We hope that you are inspired to read and explore some of the sources for yourself and see what other principles can find a home in your classroom. Some of what we present may be surprising, some dubious, but some in danger of being dismissed as 'blindingly obvious'. Before embracing or dismissing any of these principles we urge you to interrogate the evidence and think carefully about the advice we offer. While nothing works everywhere and everything might work somewhere, this is a guide to what we consider the best bets from the realm of psychology.

What Does This Look Like In The Classroom? Bridging the Gap Between Research and Practice by Carl Hendrick and Robin Macpherson

Educators around the world are uniting behind the need for the profession to have access to more high-quality research and evidence to do their job more effectively. But every year thousands of research papers are published, some of which contradict each other. How can busy teachers know which research is worth investing time in reading and understanding? And how easily is that academic research translated into excellent practice in the classroom.

In this thorough, enlightening and comprehensive book, Carl Hendrick and Robin Macpherson ask 18 of today's leading educational thinkers to distill the most up-to-date research into effective classroom practice in 10 of the most important areas of teaching.The result is a fascinating manual that will benefit every single teacher in every single school, in all four corners of the globe.

Powerful Teaching: Unleash the Science of Learning
by Pooja K. Agarwal (Author), Patrice M. Bain (Author)

Unleash powerful teaching and the science of learning in your classroom Powerful Teaching: Unleash the Science of Learning empowers educators to harness rigorous research on how students learn and unleash it in their classrooms. In this book, cognitive scientist Pooja K. Agarwal, Ph.D., and veteran K–12 teacher Patrice M. Bain, Ed.S., decipher cognitive science research and illustrate ways to successfully apply the science of learning in classrooms settings. This practical resource is filled with evidence-based strategies that are easily implemented in less than a minute—without additional prepping, grading, or funding! Research demonstrates that these powerful strategies raise student achievement by a letter grade or more; boost learning for diverse students, grade levels, and subject areas; and enhance students 'higher-order learning and transfer of knowledge beyond the classroom. Drawing on a fifteen-year scientist-teacher collaboration, more than 100 years of research on learning, and rich experiences from educators in K–12 and higher education, the authors present highly accessible step-by-step guidance on how to transform teaching with four essential strategies: Retrieval practice, spacing, interleaving, and feedback-driven metacognition. With Powerful Teaching, you will:

Develop a deep understanding of powerful teaching strategies based on the science of learning
Gain insight from real-world examples of how evidence-based strategies are being implemented in a variety of academic settings

Think critically about your current teaching practices from a research-based perspective
Develop tools to share the science of learning with students and parents, ensuring success inside and outside the classroom

Powerful Teaching: Unleash the Science of Learning is an indispensable resource for educators who want to take their instruction to the next level. Equipped with scientific knowledge and evidence-based tools, turn your teaching into powerful teaching and unleash student learning in your classroom.

The Brain-Targeted Teaching Model for 21st-Century Schools
by Mariale M. Hardiman

A powerful guide for applying brain research for more effective instruction

The Brain-Targeted Teaching Model for 21st-Century Schools serves as a bridge between research and practice by providing a cohesive, proven, and usable model of effective instruction. Compatible with other professional development programs, this model shows how to apply educational and cognitive neuroscience principles into classroom settings through a pedagogical framework. The model's six components are: (1) Establish the emotional connection to learning (2) Develop the physical learning environment(3) Design the learning experience (4) Teach for the mastery of content, skills, and concepts (5) Teach for the extension and application of knowledge(6) Evaluate learning

Welcome to Your Child's Brain: How the Mind Grows from Conception to College
by Sandra Aamodt and Sam Wang

How children think is one of the most enduring mysteries--and difficulties--of parenthood. The marketplace is full of gadgets and tools that claim to make your child smarter, happier, or learn languages faster, all built on the premise that manufacturers know something about your child's brain that you don't. These products are easy to sell, because good information about how children's minds really work is hard to come by. In their new book, neuroscientists Sandra Aamodt and Sam Wang separate fact from fiction about the inner workings of young minds. Martialing results from new studies and classic research, Aamodt and Wang provide the most complete answers out there on this subject. It liberates readers from superstitions and speculation, such as Freud's idea that all relationships are modeled on one's mother, or that it's not safe to eat sushi while pregnant. And it will reveal new truths about everything from how to make your baby sleep, to why we love to snuggle, to how children learn, forget, play, talk, walk, and feel. Welcome to Your Child's Brain is eye-opening and necessary, soon to become a staple for parents and children alike.

Uncommon Sense Teaching: Practical Insights in Brain Science to Help Students Learn
by Barbara Oakley PhD, Beth Rogowsky EdD, Terrence J. Sejnowski

Neuroscientists have made enormous strides in understanding the brain and how we learn, but little of that insight has filtered down to the way teachers teach. Uncommon Sense Teaching applies this research to the classroom for teachers, parents, and anyone interested in improving education. Topics include:
strategies for keeping students motivated and engaged, especially with online learning
helping students remember information long-term, so it isn't immediately forgotten after a test
how to teach inclusively in a diverse classroom where students have a wide range of abilities
Drawing on research findings as well as the authors 'combined decades of experience in the classroom, Uncommon Sense Teaching equips readers with the tools to enhance their teaching, whether they're seasoned professionals or parents trying to offer extra support for their children's education.

The Teaching Brain: An Evolutionary Trait at the Heart of Education
by Vanessa Rodriguez, Michelle Fitzpatrick

What is at work in the mind of a five-year-old explaining the game of tag to a new friend? What is going on in the head of a thirty-five-year-old parent showing a first-grader how to button a coat? And what exactly is happening in the brain of a sixty-five-year-old professor discussing statistics with a room full of graduate students?

While research about the nature and science of learning abounds, shockingly few insights into how and why humans teach have emerged—until now. Countering the dated yet widely held presumption that teaching is simply the transfer of knowledge from one person to another, The Teaching Brain weaves together scientific research and real-life examples to show that teaching is a dynamic interaction and an evolutionary cognitive skill that develops from birth to adulthood. With engaging, accessible prose, Harvard researcher Vanessa Rodriguez reveals what it actually takes to become an expert teacher. At a time when all sides of the teaching debate tirelessly seek to define good teaching—or even how to build a better teacher—The Teaching Brain upends the misguided premises for how we measure the success of teachers.

COURSES

How We Learn
By: Monisha Pasupathi, The Great Courses Narrated by: Monisha Pasupathi
https://www.thegreatcourses.com/courses/how-we-learn

Learning is a lifelong adventure.It starts in your mother's womb, accelerates to high speed in infancy and childhood, and continues through every age. Whether you're actively engaged in mastering a new skill, intuitively discovering an unfamiliar place, or even sleeping - which is fundamental to helping you consolidate and hold on to what you've learned - you are truly born to learn around the clock. But few of us know how we learn, which is the key to learning and studying more effectively.This series of 24 vibrant and accessible lectures has been designed to change that. Designed by an award-winning psychology teacher and expert on how people of all ages master new skills and information, it sheds light on what's going on when we learn and dispels common myths about the subject.Professor Pasupathi's many examples cover the modern history of research on learning, from behaviorist theory in the early 20th century to the most recent debates about whether IQ can be separated from achievement - and even whether a spectrum of different learning styles and multiple intelligences really exists.The lectures are also a rich source of readily implemented tips on how to excel in many different learning situations, including mastering difficult material, motivating children to learn, and preserving learning aptitude as we grow older.

The Learning Brain

By: The Great Courses Narrated by: Professor Thad A. Polk PhD Carnegie Mellon University

https://www.thegreatcourses.com/courses/the-learning-brain

One of the most complicated and advanced computers on Earth can't be purchased in any store. This astonishing device, responsible for storing and retrieving vast quantities of information that can be accessed at a moment's notice, is the human brain. How does such a dynamic and powerful machine make memories, learn a language, and remember how to drive a car? What habits can we adopt in order to learn more effectively throughout our lives? And how do external factors like traumatic injuries and mood affect our gray matter? The answers to these questions are merely the tip of the iceberg in The Learning Brain.These 24 half-hour lectures offer in-depth and surprising lessons about how the brain learns and how we can optimize that learning. Begin your journey by focusing on which parts of the brain are responsible for different kinds of memory, from personal experiences and memorized facts to short-term memory, and how these systems work on a psychological and biological level. Then, discover how to better absorb and retain all kinds of memories in all stages of life. This course is chock-full of valuable information, whether you're learning a new language at 60 or discovering calculus at 16. If you need better study habits, struggle with learning a new skill, or just worry about memories fading with age, The Learning Brain will provide illuminating insights.Take this journey with Thad Polk, professor of psychology at the University of Michigan, whose well-organized curriculum and relaxed teaching style ease you into intricate aspects of learning science, including the underlying cognitive and neural mechanisms involved. Professor Polk's credentials in psychology and over 20 years' experience in education shine through every lecture of The Learning Brain as he firmly supports this rigorous exploration with scientific studies conducted over the last several decades of neuroscientific research.

Learning How to Learn: Powerful mental tools to help you master tough subjects
https://www.coursera.org/learn/learning-how-to-learn

This course gives you easy access to the invaluable learning techniques used by experts in art, music, literature, math, science, sports, and many other disciplines. We'll learn about how the brain uses two very different learning modes and how it encapsulates ("chunks") information. We'll also cover illusions of learning, memory techniques, dealing with procrastination, and best practices shown by research to be most effective in helping you master tough subjects.

Using these approaches, no matter what your skill levels in topics you would like to master, you can change your thinking and change your life. If you're already an expert, this peep under the mental hood will give you ideas for turbocharging successful learning, including counter-intuitive test-taking tips and insights that will help you make the best use of your time on homework and problem sets. If you're struggling, you'll see a structured treasure trove of practical techniques that walk you through what you need to do to get on track. If you've ever wanted to become better at anything, this course will help serve as your guide. This course can be taken independent of, concurrent with, or prior to, its companion course, Mindshift. (Learning How to Learn is more learning-focused, and Mindshift is more career-focused.) A related course by the same instructors is Uncommon Sense Teaching.

Teachers College: The Science of Learning - What Every Teacher Should Know
https://www.edx.org/learn/social-science/teachers-college-the-science-of-learning-what-every-teacher-should

This education course will show you, through current research, how we learn — the way our brain makes, stores, and retrieves memories.
You will examine common misconceptions and

misunderstandings about learning that can prevent students from learning at their fullest capacity. Along the way you will explore the practical implications of cognitive science for classroom teaching in terms of choosing effective instructional strategies, developing useful assessments, motivating student effort, and designing learner-centered curricular units.

This course is aimed to enhance the practice of K-12 teachers.

TEACHERS COLLEGE RESOURCES

Harvard University Online Resources: The Science of Learning
https://bokcenter.harvard.edu/science-learning

https://www.gse.harvard.edu/ideas/usable-knowledge/20/04/applied-science-learning

Johns Hopkins University: Science of learning institute

https://hub.jhu.edu/tags/science-learning-institute/articles/

www.ingramcontent.com/pod-product-compliance
Lightning Source LLC
LaVergne TN
LVHW022324080426
835508LV00013BA/1314